DEADLY DISEASES AND EPIDEMICS

HEPATITIS

Lyle W. Horn

CONSULTING EDITOR
The Late **I. Edward Alcamo**
Distinguished Teaching Professor of Microbiology,
SUNY Farmingdale

FOREWORD BY
David Heymann
World Health Organization

CHELSEA HOUSE
P U B L I S H E R S
A Haights Cross Communications

Philadelph

Dedication

We dedicate the books in the DEADLY DISEASES AND EPIDEMICS series to Ed Alcamo, whose wit, charm, intelligence, and commitment to biology education were second to none.

CHELSEA HOUSE PUBLISHERS

VP, NEW PRODUCT DEVELOPMENT Sally Cheney
DIRECTOR OF PRODUCTION Kim Shinners
CREATIVE MANAGER Takeshi Takahashi
MANUFACTURING MANAGER Diann Grasse

Staff for Hepatitis

EXECUTIVE EDITOR Tara Koellhoffer
ASSOCIATE EDITOR Beth Reger
EDITORIAL ASSISTANT Kuorkor Dzani
PRODUCTION EDITOR Noelle Nardone
PHOTO EDITOR Sarah Bloom
SERIES DESIGNER Terry Mallon
COVER DESIGNER Keith Trego
LAYOUT 21st Century Publishing and Communications, Inc.

A Haights Cross Communications ✦ Company ®

http://www.chelseahouse.com

First Printing

1 3 5 7 9 8 6 4 2

Library of Congress Cataloging-in-Publication Data

Horne, Lyle W.
  Hepatitis / Lyle W. Horn.
    p. cm.—(Deadly diseases and epidemics)
  Includes bibliographical references.
    ISBN 0-7910-6702-5 — ISBN 0-7910-8378-0 (pbk.)
  1. Hepatitis. I. Title. II. Series.
RC848.H42H67 2005
616.3'623—dc22

                                                    2004026180

All links and web addresses were checked and verified to be correct at the time of publication. Because of the dynamic nature of the web, some addresses and links may have changed since publication and may no longer be valid.

Table of Contents

Foreword

In the 1960s, many of the infectious diseases that had terrorized generations were tamed. After a century of advances, the leading killers of Americans both young and old were being prevented with new vaccines or cured with new medicines. The risk of death from pneumonia, tuberculosis (TB), meningitis, influenza, whooping cough, and diphtheria declined dramatically. New vaccines lifted the fear that summer would bring polio, and a global campaign was on the verge of eradicating smallpox worldwide. New pesticides like DDT cleared mosquitoes from homes and fields, thus reducing the incidence of malaria, which was present in the southern United States and which remains a leading killer of children worldwide. New technologies produced safe drinking water and removed the risk of cholera and other water-borne diseases. Science seemed unstoppable. Disease seemed destined to all but disappear.

But the euphoria of the 1960s has evaporated.

The microbes fought back. Those causing diseases like TB and malaria evolved resistance to cheap and effective drugs. The mosquito developed the ability to defuse pesticides. New diseases emerged, including AIDS, Legionnaires, and Lyme disease. And diseases which had not been seen in decades re-emerged, as the hantavirus did in the Navajo Nation in 1993. Technology itself actually created new health risks. The global transportation network, for example, meant that diseases like West Nile virus could spread beyond isolated regions and quickly become global threats. Even modern public health protections sometimes failed, as they did in 1993 in Milwaukee, Wisconsin, resulting in 400,000 cases of the digestive system illness cryptosporidiosis. And, more recently, the threat from smallpox, a disease believed to be completely eradicated, has returned along with other potential bioterrorism weapons such as anthrax.

The lesson is that the fight against infectious diseases will never end.

In our constant struggle against disease, we as individuals have a weapon that does not require vaccines or drugs, and that is the warehouse of knowledge. We learn from the history of science that "modern" beliefs can be wrong. In this series of books, for example, you will learn that diseases like syphilis were once thought to be caused by eating potatoes. The invention of the microscope set science on the right path. There are more positive lessons from history. For example, smallpox was eliminated by vaccinating everyone who had come in contact with an infected person. This "ring" approach to smallpox control is still the preferred method for confronting an outbreak, should the disease be intentionally reintroduced.

At the same time, we are constantly adding new drugs, new vaccines, and new information to the warehouse. Recently, the entire human genome was decoded. So too was the genome of the parasite that causes malaria. Perhaps by looking at the microbe and the victim through the lens of genetics we will be able to discover new ways to fight malaria, which remains the leading killer of children in many countries.

Because of advances in our understanding of such diseases as AIDS, entire new classes of anti-retroviral drugs have been developed. But resistance to all these drugs has already been detected, so we know that AIDS drug development must continue.

Education, experimentation, and the discoveries that grow out of them are the best tools to protect health. Opening this book may put you on the path of discovery. I hope so, because new vaccines, new antibiotics, new technologies, and, most importantly, new scientists are needed now more than ever if we are to remain on the winning side of this struggle against microbes.

David Heymann
Executive Director
Communicable Diseases Section
World Health Organization
Geneva, Switzerland

1

Introduction to Hepatitis

About 500 million people throughout the world are infected by one of six hepatitis viruses. This disease causes much suffering and has many unique features. But what is hepatitis?

Hepatitis is an **inflammation** of the liver (in Latin, *hepaticus* means "of the liver") caused either by a toxic (poisonous or harmful) substance or by a viral infection (Figure 1.1). Besides causing direct damage to the liver, toxic substances can also aggravate a viral infection. An example of a toxic substance is alcohol. Taken in moderation, alcohol is regarded as safe, but when abused or taken along with some medications, or when taken by people who have certain diseases, it can cause complications. For instance, even just a little alcohol consumed by a person who has viral hepatitis can rapidly cause severe liver damage. This book discusses only viral hepatitides (plural of *hepatitis*) because these diseases are of major importance for public health worldwide and because their causes have one thing in common—viral infection.

Five different viruses—designated A, B, C, D, and E—are known to cause hepatitis; a sixth virus, G, is associated with hepatitis but has not been shown to cause serious **clinical disease**. There have even been some reports of a seventh virus, F. These reports are not confirmed, and health experts do not accept it as a unique virus.

All forms of viral hepatitis have common symptoms (discussed in Chapter 2), but each also has its own special features. Recognizing these features helps us understand how the disease is transmitted, how it affects us, how it can be treated, and how we can prevent it.

Let's start by introducing Mike, who has come down with a form of hepatitis. Later, you will also read the stories of Rhonda, who contracted

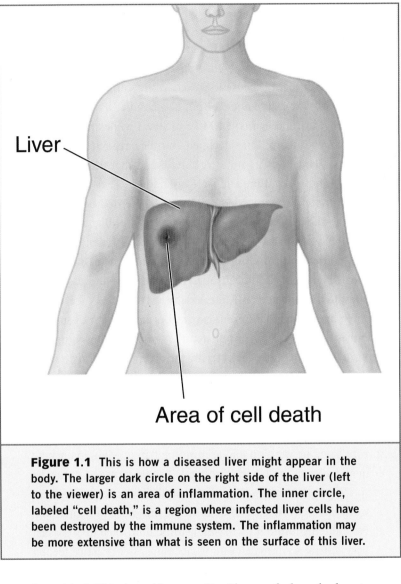

Liver

Area of cell death

Figure 1.1 This is how a diseased liver might appear in the body. The larger dark circle on the right side of the liver (left to the viewer) is an area of inflammation. The inner circle, labeled "cell death," is a region where infected liver cells have been destroyed by the immune system. The inflammation may be more extensive than what is seen on the surface of this liver.

hepatitis A; Valerie and her son, David, one of whom had acute and the other chronic hepatitis B; Kevin, who developed acute hepatitis C; and Satya, who acquired hepatitis E. Each had experiences that were both similar to and very different from Mike's experiences.

MIKE

Mike was a junior at a large high school and a starting forward on the soccer team. Near the end of his junior year, he met some cousins of a buddy at a party. He spent a lot of time talking with them because they were really into music and had friends who were members of popular bands. As the party was winding down, they invited Mike to stay a while and do some cocaine with them. Mike declined, but they assured him that it was not dangerous if you were careful and that they had been doing it for a long time and were not addicts. They really raved about the experience. Mike was curious. He had developed a trust in these guys and so he agreed to try it. Mike, his friend, and the two cousins gathered around the kitchen table. Cocaine was poured out into four lines on the table. Each young man inhaled (snorted) his line through a special straw and passed the straw to the next person. Mike was the last to snort. Mike felt the surge his friends told him to expect, but he found it disturbing rather than pleasurable. He hated the sense of losing control of himself. He felt guilty about trying the drug and had no desire to do it again. It was just a stupid experiment that he tried in a weak moment, he reasoned. So Mike went on with his life.

Mike had a great summer. He went to soccer camp, where he learned new ball-handling techniques and defensive maneuvers. Then he went on a long camping trip in Montana, where he did a lot of hiking and fishing. When he returned home, he was eager to start his senior year and play soccer. The team workouts went well for Mike until the first week of September. He suddenly found it increasingly difficult to keep up his usual pace during scrimmages and went home after practice feeling really tired. He also began to have a hard time getting up for school in the morning and felt exhausted all day. His coach noticed the change in Mike. Mike's soccer play had become so poor that the coach didn't start him in the first game. The coach knew this tiredness was not normal for Mike, so he urged Mike to see a doctor and he called Mike's parents.

Mike's doctor talked with him for a long time to get some clues about the cause of the unusual fatigue. When a patient complains of fatigue and has no other symptoms, a diagnosis can be very difficult to make. Sixty or more medical conditions have fatigue as a major symptom. Most of these diseases could be ruled out for Mike based on his general condition and medical history. Mike's doctor knew that he had been immunized for hepatitis A and hepatitis B as a young child. So Mike was checked for some other diseases that cause serious fatigue. He was tested for Lyme disease because he had spent so much time outdoors and might have been bitten by an infected deer tick, but the test result was negative. His thyroid gland was also checked and found to be normal. Mike's muscle strength was excellent, his heart was healthy, his blood pressure was fine, he did not have diabetes or infectious mononucleosis, and he was not anemic (having low levels of iron in the blood). Fatigue is associated with all of these diseases, but none affected Mike; he just felt tired.

When his doctor asked whether he had ever used drugs, Mike was embarrassed and did not answer honestly. After all, he had only experimented with cocaine once. The doctor asked if he had had a blood transfusion or been stuck with a syringe needle within the past year. Had he been tattooed or had his ears pierced? All the answers were no. Mike thought these were weird questions, but the doctor was trying to determine whether Mike might have been exposed to viruses that are present in the blood and can infect the body only by direct entry into the blood.

Viruses that infect through the blood are referred to as **bloodborne**, and their transmission, which occurs by any route other than through the intestines, is referred to as **parenteral transmission**. Common parenteral routes include puncture by an object contaminated by a virus such as a needle, or direct exposure of an open wound or sore to an object contaminated with blood.

Poor countries are likely to have water contaminated by human feces. Many viruses are passed out of the body (shed) in the stool and can be transmitted through a simple act such as eating fresh vegetables that were washed with contaminated water. Consumption of contaminated water or food allows these viruses to enter the body from the gut. This route of transmission is referred to as **enteric** (relating to the intestine). Mike had not traveled to an underdeveloped country with poor sanitation. The doctor had no reason to suspect that Mike was lying to him, but he decided to check for hepatitis just in case Mike had unknowingly been exposed to contaminated blood or other body fluids, contaminated water, or fresh foods washed with contaminated water.

The first tests for viral hepatitis are serological (pertaining to blood serum). **Serum** is the liquid part of whole blood that remains after all blood cells and clotting materials are removed. When a person is infected by a **microbe** (a microorganism that does not have a nucleus), **proteins** (large functional and structural molecules in cells and body fluids) called **antigens**, which are made by the microbe, are found in the serum. These signal the presence of a foreign substance to the immune system. Other proteins called **antibodies** are produced by the immune system in response to antigens and may also be present in the blood. Antigens and the antibodies made to fight the foreign microbe are specific. That is, a particular microbe antigen is not found on any other microbe, and the antibodies produced in response to the antigen recognize only that antigen. It is these substances that are detected by serological tests. These tests may be followed by other tests for proteins that are released from injured liver cells and for **viral nucleic acid** that is specific to a virus. Finally, a **liver biopsy** (sampling of liver tissue) may be done to determine the extent of liver damage. (We will review these tests and discuss the immune response in Chapter 4.)

It turned out that Mike's serological test results were positive for acute hepatitis. Fatigue is the only symptom that Mike experienced. His fatigue became so bad that he had to quit the soccer team and his schoolwork deteriorated.

There is no treatment that can cure acute hepatitis. All doctors can do is treat the symptoms. Mike was advised to get lots of rest, to eat properly, to refrain from alcohol under any circumstances because it can aggravate the disease and cause liver failure very rapidly, and avoid strenuous exercise until he felt better. He was also instructed about how to prevent spreading his disease to his family and others. Mike was referred to a liver disease specialist who would assess Mike's status regularly.

Mike slowly recovered his stamina over a period of 6 months, although his energy level was not what it once was. He was able to improve his schoolwork and participate in normal social activities, but he had to forget about sports during his senior year. We will revisit Mike's case in Chapter 11.

2

The Phases of Hepatitis and Their Common Symptoms

Acute viral hepatitis is the initial short-term stage of the disease. It begins with the entry of the virus into the body and continues for up to six months. Mike's experience was typical of a person in an **acute** phase of hepatitis. All forms of viral hepatitis (A to E) have an acute phase. Symptoms may or may not appear during this phase. Mike had only one symptom—fatigue—and was lucky to have it because it made early diagnosis possible.

Chronic hepatitis refers to a continuing lifelong infection. The diagnosis of chronic hepatitis is made only when the **clinical signs** (abnormalities that can be discovered by examination) and **symptoms** (abnormalities that are sensed by the patient) have lasted more than six months. Hepatitis viruses B, C, and D are known to cause chronic hepatitis; the others do not. Chronic hepatitis does not always develop because a person's immune system may successfully defeat the virus. But it can develop when a person's immune system is unable to eliminate the invading virus. When the virus avoids detection by not producing proteins (antigens) that allow the immune system to recognize it as an invader or by constantly changing (mutating) the antigens it produces or by reproducing faster than the immune system is able to attack and destroy the virus, chronic hepatitis can occur. Symptoms may first appear, continue, or disappear during the chronic phase. Sometimes they come and go. The absence of symptoms does not mean there is no disease. It is not understood why the symptoms of hepatitis are erratic.

Some people infected with hepatitis don't experience any symptoms until late in the chronic phase (20 or more years after infection). This symptom-free experience is most common during the acute phase in infants and young children, but it can also be possible for adults. The reasons why a person is symptom-free are not understood, but the fact that symptom-free disease occurs is important for the welfare of the patient and for public health.

Infected people who are symptom-free may discover only by chance that they have been infected. Doctors do not check for hepatitis during routine physical examinations. However, all donated blood is checked for hepatitis A, B, and C, so a blood donor may receive a letter from the Red Cross or a local hospital informing him or her of the presence of hepatitis infection. Life insurance companies often require tests for hepatitis before issuing a policy to an applicant. A person may go to the doctor complaining of flu-like symptoms, and the doctor may decide to check for hepatitis when no influenza infection is found. The patient may then learn that he or she has viral hepatitis.

The severity of symptoms varies a great deal among individuals with viral hepatitis. Some people never have symptoms. When symptoms do occur, not all known symptoms are necessarily experienced. Some people experience only mild flu-like discomfort and go about their daily lives without interruption. Others see a physician and have to rest in bed for a few days to several weeks. In rare cases, a person has to be hospitalized. Although there are exceptions, the older a person is when infected, the more likely he or she is to have serious symptoms. The reasons why this is true are not understood. Possibly, as we age, our immune system becomes less effective.

There is no treatment that can rid our bodies entirely of hepatitis virus infection. Only our own immune system can defeat the virus. When the immune system defeats a viral infection, it is said that the disease is **self-limited**. Medical treatment is directed toward relief of discomfort and symptoms and toward compensation for changes in body functions that could cause death. Reduction of fever, replacement of body fluids and intravenous feeding, and support of breathing with a respirator are examples of the support that may be required. A liver transplant is an extreme last resort in some cases.

A PUBLIC HEALTH PROBLEM

Communicable diseases that are symptom-free are a serious public health problem. A person who is unaware of being infected may spread the disease widely. Virus-infected, symptom-free people who have had the disease for at least 6 months are called "carriers" of the virus. One of the most common ways that hepatitis was transmitted in the past was by blood transfusion. Unaware of his or her hepatitis infection, a carrier would donate blood, which would then be given to someone in need. Viral hepatitis would then develop very quickly, sometimes within a week of the transfusion, and place patients who were already seriously ill at great risk. It has become routine in developed countries to screen donated blood for hepatitis B since about 1972, when an economical and reliable test became available, and for hepatitis C since 1992. Screening is routine only in developed countries, however, because the cost is too high and laboratory facilities are not available in many poor countries. The incidence of hepatitis after blood transfusion in developed countries fell markedly after blood screening began. According to the Centers for Disease Control and Prevention (CDC), in the 1980s before blood screening began, there was an average of 242,000 new hepatitis C infections per year in the United States, but the number dropped to 36,000 per year by 1996, 4 years after routine blood screening began.

ACUTE PHASES OF INFECTION

Acute viral hepatitis can be divided into four phases. The **incubation phase** begins with the initial infection and continues until the onset of symptoms or, if no symptoms appear, until blood tests show that the person's immune system has begun to fight the virus. This phase can last from one week to many months, depending on the kind of virus and the number of viral microbes the person was infected with. The larger the dose of these microbes, the shorter the incubation period. Hepatitis after blood transfusion, for example, develops within a week because the viral dose received by transfusion is very large. (Mike's incubation period was about 4 months.) During this phase, the virus reproduces rapidly and the infected person may be highly contagious. This period is dangerous for others because the infected person does not know about the infection and cannot take precautions to avoid passing it on.

The **prodromal phase** starts with the onset of symptoms, although we know that not all people experience symptoms. In Mike's case, the symptom was fatigue. A person may think he or she has a mild case of the flu, which may include a low-grade fever. This may be followed within days by anorexia (loss of appetite), malaise (feeling "down" with fatigue and no energy), and nausea and vomiting. Smokers often lose their desire to smoke.

During the prodromal phase, the blood levels of some proteins that are made by the liver rise. This is because the body's immune response to the virus actually causes damage to liver cells. One of the most important of these proteins is an enzyme called **alanine aminotransferase** or **ALT**. ALT is involved in the normal chemical processing of the amino acid alanine. It converts alanine to carbon dioxide and water and provides useful energy for the cell. Doctors may monitor the blood levels of ALT in a patient they know has hepatitis to follow the progress of the infection. However, a single measurement of blood ALT cannot provide diagnostic evidence of hepatitis.

Three to 10 days after the first symptoms of hepatitis appear, the **icteric phase** of infection may begin. The word *icteric* means "jaundiced" and refers to changes in the color of urine, stools, skin, and sclerae (whites of the eyes). The urine may turn very dark yellow at first. The stools may become pale or light yellow or may be described as clay-like. Yellow skin may not be obvious, but often yellowing can be seen underneath

ENZYMES

Enzymes are proteins that carry out very specific chemical reactions in the cell with high efficiency and speed. A chemical reaction is a process by which two or more different chemicals interact to form new chemicals. Many chemical reactions in the body could not occur, or would proceed too slowly for practical use, without the aid of enzymes. They are essential for normal cell function. Thousands of enzymes are known, and each one is dedicated to a single chemical reaction. One seemingly simple process, such as the conversion of a sugar molecule to carbon dioxide and water, can actually involve about two dozen separate chemical reactions, each requiring a specific enzyme. Enzymes are required to make nucleic acids (DNA and RNA) and proteins; to make amino acids, which are the building blocks of all proteins; to manufacture or destroy a long list of chemical substances; to make our muscles shorten and develop force; and to facilitate many other essential processes that are too numerous to list. Not all enzymes are found in every cell of our body. Cells make only the enzymes they need to perform their specific functions. Alanine aminotransferase (ALT) is an important enzyme for normal liver function, for example, but is not very important in a skin or muscle cell. When a cell is sick or dying, enzymes leak out of the cell and into the blood. Knowledge of the blood level of an enzyme such as ALT can give clues to the degree of cell damage that has occurred in an organ that is known to use that enzyme.

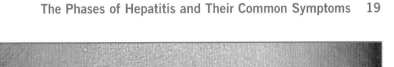

Figure 2.1 This young man has jaundice. This is a very good example of the "yellowing" caused by jaundice. The sclerae (whites of the eyes) are obviously yellow. Healthy "whites" of the eyes are truly white. This feature stands out most prominently in this person. A closer look will show that his skin, especially his nose and around the eyes, has a yellow tone. An even closer look will show that the moist tissues on the edges of his lower eyelids are also yellowed. These tissues are normally pink.

the fingernails or in the sclerae (Figure 2.1). Most people with hepatitis do not develop **jaundice**, but it is still common enough that it is considered an important symptom. During the icteric phase, the symptoms that appeared during the earlier prodromal phase may fade and be replaced by itching on the body trunk. The jaundice itself is at its worst about 1 to 2 weeks after the start of the icteric phase, and then usually fades over a period of 4 to 8 weeks.

Eventually, if the infection is self-limited, the immune system begins to win the battle against the virus and ultimately triumphs. This is the final phase of acute hepatitis, the **recovery phase**, which typically lasts 4 to 8 weeks but can last up to 6 months. Symptoms slowly fade away, including jaundice.

BILIRUBIN

The cause of yellowing or jaundice is an excess of the chemical bilirubin in blood and urine. **Bilirubin** is a product of the breakdown of red blood cells. Red blood cells contain hemoglobin, which is a protein whose primary function is to bind oxygen for transport from the lungs to the rest of the body. The key part of hemoglobin for binding oxygen is called the heme group. The heme group contains one iron ion. Bilirubin is a remnant of the heme group without the iron ion that results from the destruction of hemoglobin. It is normally taken up from the blood by the liver, modified chemically, and excreted by way of the bile into the small intestine and thus in the feces. Modified bilirubin is further changed to other chemicals in the gut such as stercobilinogen, which gives the normal stool its typical brown color. In a normal adult, about 0.2 grams (g) of bilirubin is excreted in the stool every day.

When liver cells are not functioning properly, release of modified bilirubin may be impaired. Considerable amounts of bilirubin are not taken up at all by the liver, and modified bilirubin is released back to the blood. As a consequence, the modified and unmodified bilirubin build up in the blood. Both of these chemicals have a yellow color. The excess bilirubin can move out of the blood into the tissues, where it causes yellow discoloration, and is excreted by the kidney into the urine, which accounts for the dark yellow color of urine during jaundice. Reduced excretion of bilirubin into the gut during liver disease results in less stercobilinogen, or brown pigment, and a lighter-colored stool.

During this phase, the liver may be enlarged (**hepatomegaly**) and tender to the touch, so that a person may feel discomfort just below the right ribs with slight pressure. Fatigue may be the last symptom to disappear. Finally, all symptoms disappear, and the person returns to normal health with immunity to future infections by the same kind of virus. **Immunity** means that the immune system remembers the specific antigens of a microbe and can be reactivated quickly to fight a new invasion by that organism. Antibodies may also remain in the blood indefinitely, so that they can immediately attack any reinvasion.

COMPLICATIONS OF THE ACUTE PHASE

A rare and fatal complication that can develop during the acute phase of hepatitis is known as **fulminant hepatitis.** *Fulminant* means sudden and explosive, like a lightning strike. This complication is most often associated with hepatitis B (1% of cases), but can also develop with hepatitides A and C. Death can occur within 2 weeks of onset. It is not understood how fulminant hepatitis develops, and there is no cure. Liver cells are destroyed very rapidly and liver size decreases dramatically (known as acute yellow atrophy). The liver ceases to provide essential functions for the rest of the body, and toxic substances build up in the blood. These toxic materials enter the brain and cause **hepatic encephalopathy,** a disorder of the brain caused by a malfunctioning liver. An irreversible coma can develop within hours. The pressure of fluids in the brain builds up and causes physical damage to brain cells directly and reduces blood flow to the brain. This results in additional brain cell damage and death due to lack of oxygen. The toxic substances can also promote kidney failure, which is always fatal. However, in some cases that are caught early enough, a liver transplant may save the patient's life. Survival generally is not common; it is most likely in children and extremely rare in adults. A lucky few recover completely, have no permanent damage to the liver or brain, and have no chronic viral infection.

CHRONIC PHASES OF INFECTION

Chronic hepatitis begins after six months of infection without recovery. Chronic hepatitis can be divided into three phases. The first is the **replicative phase**, during which the virus reproduces itself actively and infects healthy liver cells. This phase can last several years, resulting in a large amount of virus in the blood (**viremia**). The disease is most contagious during this phase. The **seroconversion phase** follows the replicative phase. During this phase, the immune system attacks and destroys about 10% of infected liver cells each year. Usually, an infected person has no symptoms during the seroconversion phase and the person also has less viremia, although blood levels of ALT are high because of the destruction of liver cells. Finally, the **nonreplicative phase** sets in, during which the virus stops reproducing and viremia is minimal. However, replication may be reactivated at any time for reasons that are not understood.

The symptoms of chronic viral hepatitis include those suffered in the acute phase. They may come and go and often are not as severe as in the acute phase, but there will always be some degree of viremia. A person may be symptom-free for many years. Others may suffer from persistent symptoms, especially fatigue. Jaundice may reappear and, if it does, it is considered a serious sign of advanced disease. Hepatomegaly (an enlarged liver) may persist or get worse. Some people may live a normal lifespan without serious consequences. In others, the disease progresses very slowly to a stage in which liver failure may cause death. The likelihood of this happening depends on which hepatitis virus the person is infected with and whether the infection is properly treated. In the United States, infection with hepatitis C virus is most likely to lead to death because the treatments for hepatitis C are not highly effective compared with treatment for hepatitis B.

About 70% of deaths caused by chronic hepatitis in the United States are caused by hepatitis C.

COMPLICATIONS OF THE CHRONIC PHASE

The first serious complication that may develop in the chronic phase of hepatitis, 10 or more years after infection, is cirrhosis. **Cirrhosis** is end-stage liver disease and has many possible causes—chronic viral hepatitis being one and alcohol abuse being the most common. *End-stage* means the end of life. About 10% to 20% of chronic hepatitis cases lead to cirrhosis. *Cirrhosis* means "yellow condition" and refers to the dull orange-yellow appearance of the diseased liver, which is caused in this case by deposits of large amounts of fat. There is massive damage to liver cells, caused mainly by the immune system's unrelenting attempt to eliminate the virus. Immune cells called killer T cells attack and destroy the infected liver cells rather than destroying the virus directly. In this way, the body attacks itself. As a result, the body attempts to repair the damaged liver cells by forming scar tissue in the liver. This reaction is similar to scab formation after an injury to the skin. In turn, the blood supply to many parts of the organ is disrupted by the scarring, leading to loss of function and further cell death. Cirrhosis ranks third as a cause of death in the Western world, after heart disease and cancer, in people aged 45 to 65 years and 12th as a cause of death among people of all ages. There is no cure for cirrhosis. A liver transplant may be life-saving if the person's overall condition has not deteriorated too much and a suitable donor can be found.

A second serious complication in chronic hepatitis, which usually develops more slowly and appears later than cirrhosis, is a liver cancer known as **hepatocellular carcinoma**. The name simply means that the cancer arises from the liver cells themselves (the **hepatocytes**). Having cirrhosis is thought to greatly increase the risk of cancer, but it is not necessary for cancer to occur. Hepatocellular carcinoma is incurable and fatal and is most likely to occur in people with the chronic hepatitides B and C who are between 35 and 65 years old. About 30% of cases of chronic hepatitis B and 10% of cases of chronic hepatitis C proceed to liver cancer. In these cases, a liver transplant may be life-saving.

There is a vaccine available for prevention of hepatitis B. This vaccine is the first one of just a few vaccines that actually can prevent a cancer, which it does by preventing hepatitis B.

In summary, viral hepatitis has both an acute phase, which develops in everyone who gets infected, and a chronic phase, which does not always develop and occurs only with the hepatitis B, C, and D viruses. The acute phase typically lasts 6 months or less, whereas the chronic phase may last a lifetime. The most common symptoms are malaise or fatigue, low-grade fever, jaundice, and nausea and vomiting. Most cases of hepatitis are resolved by the end of the acute phase because the immune system successfully eliminates the virus. These infections are self-limited. A person is then immune to another infection by the same virus. An infected person in the chronic phase may never experience symptoms or may do so only very late in life. In others, symptoms may come and go, or they may be persistent, especially fatigue. Chronic hepatitis may progress after 10 or more years to cirrhosis and after 20 or more years to liver cancer. Both complications are usually fatal, although a liver transplant may save the life of the person infected.

3

Looking at the Liver

UNIQUENESS OF THE LIVER

The liver is the largest organ by weight in the body. The average weight of the liver in a healthy adult is about 3 pounds (1.36 kg). This remarkable organ performs many functions that are essential for life. One of its amazing properties is its ability to **regenerate** (rebuild and restore to its original structure and function). It is the only human organ that can do this when a large amount of tissue is involved. If some of the liver is removed surgically, the remaining liver can regrow to its original size and function normally. It is also true that the liver can lose 75% of its cells before it stops functioning. This fact is extremely important for understanding the long-term, or chronic, effects of viral hepatitis. We will review these functions below.

The liver is found in the upper third of the abdomen. It rests on the stomach, the intestines, and the right kidney. It is divided into two large subunits (Figure 3.1) called **lobes**. The right lobe is the larger of the two and is separated from the left lobe by a large ligament (falciform ligament) that also attaches the liver to the diaphragm and abdominal wall. Both of these lobes are closest to the diaphragm. There are two other lobes that are small and are located underneath the major lobes: the caudate lobe and the quadrate lobe (Figure 3.2). Four other ligaments also attach the lobes to the abdominal wall. The normal liver is dark red-brown in color.

The liver is supplied by the **hepatic artery**, which provides the oxygenated blood the liver needs, and the hepatic and **portal veins**. The portal vein delivers all of the blood that flows through the intestines to the liver. This blood carries all the nutrients that have been recovered from the intestines. Everything we eat or ingest that can enter the blood

(continued on page 27)

25

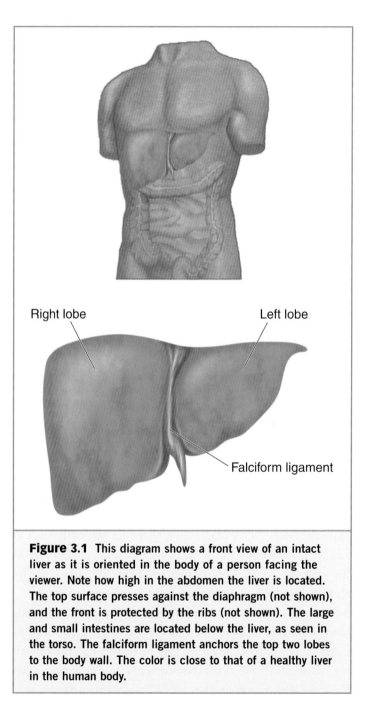

Right lobe

Left lobe

Falciform ligament

Figure 3.1 This diagram shows a front view of an intact liver as it is oriented in the body of a person facing the viewer. Note how high in the abdomen the liver is located. The top surface presses against the diaphragm (not shown), and the front is protected by the ribs (not shown). The large and small intestines are located below the liver, as seen in the torso. The falciform ligament anchors the top two lobes to the body wall. The color is close to that of a healthy liver in the human body.

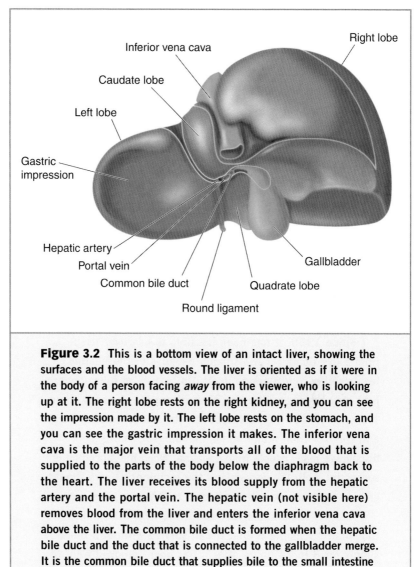

Inferior vena cava

Caudate lobe

Left lobe

Gastric impression

Right lobe

Hepatic artery
Portal vein
Common bile duct

Gallbladder

Quadrate lobe

Round ligament

Figure 3.2 This is a bottom view of an intact liver, showing the surfaces and the blood vessels. The liver is oriented as if it were in the body of a person facing *away* from the viewer, who is looking up at it. The right lobe rests on the right kidney, and you can see the impression made by it. The left lobe rests on the stomach, and you can see the gastric impression it makes. The inferior vena cava is the major vein that transports all of the blood that is supplied to the parts of the body below the diaphragm back to the heart. The liver receives its blood supply from the hepatic artery and the portal vein. The hepatic vein (not visible here) removes blood from the liver and enters the inferior vena cava above the liver. The common bile duct is formed when the hepatic bile duct and the duct that is connected to the gallbladder merge. It is the common bile duct that supplies bile to the small intestine (not shown).

(continued from page 25)

must first flow through the liver. Portal blood accounts for 80% of the blood supplied to the liver, with the artery supplying the rest. The **hepatic vein** collects all the blood supplied to the liver

LIVER TRANSPLANTS

Liver transplants are performed only with patients who have no other hope for survival and who meet strict technical requirements that ensure a good chance for success. The liver is the second most frequently transplanted organ (after the kidney) and the procedure has become common throughout the developed world. About 17,000 patients are eligible for a transplant every year in the United States, but only about 5,300 procedures are performed because of the limited number of donors. Usually, donors have died from causes that have not affected their livers, such as an automobile accident. Of course, these people must have completed an organ donor form or have relatives who are willing to grant permission for donation. In addition, the donor must have the same blood type and be of similar body size as the recipient.

Since 1999, it has been possible to use liver tissue from a live donor for transplants because of the healthy liver's ability to regenerate itself. Up to 50% of a live donor's liver may be taken. The risk of death for the donor is about 1 chance in 100 (1%). Moreover, the donor must undergo and recover from major abdominal surgery. These facts discourage many people from donating. When the procedure is successful, both the donor's and the recipient's livers should grow to normal size within about 6 to 8 weeks after surgery.

Another remarkable fact about the liver that makes transplants feasible is that it can survive without a blood supply for 8 to 24 hours after it has been removed from the body. This means that the donor and recipient may live on opposite sides of the country without causing a problem for the procedure. Transplant surgeons prefer to use livers that have been out of the body for less than 8 hours, but will use older ones if necessary.

and returns it to the heart. At any instant, about 13% of the body's blood is in the liver. The hepatic **bile duct** is another important tube that leaves the liver. This tube collects all the **bile** produced by the liver and delivers it to the small intestine just beyond the stomach. Attached to the bile duct is the gallbladder, which serves as a storage reservoir for bile when it is not needed in the gut for digestion of fats. About half of the bile produced by the liver first goes into the gallbladder. When we eat fatty food, the fat triggers a reflex that causes the gallbladder to contract and push the stored bile into the gut to help absorb the fats from the gut into the blood.

The bile duct system is like a highly branched tree. The smallest vessels, **canaliculi**, are microscopic in size and are present throughout the liver. They gradually converge into larger and larger vessels, just as the small branches of a tree converge into ever-larger branches, until finally the "trunk of the tree," or hepatic bile duct, is reached. This is a very efficient system for collecting bile from the liver cells.

The liver lobes are further subdivided into many thousands of basic functional units or small lobes called **lobules**. Lobules can only be seen clearly with a microscope. Figure 3.3 is a sketch of a typical lobule. When we look at a cross-section of a lobule, we can see a hexagonal (six-sided) boundary, a central hub or axle, and lots of "spokes" radiating between the hub and the periphery of the lobule. Open spaces between the spokes are called **sinusoids**, which means "small sinuses." A **sinus** is a cavity, channel, or hollow.

At each of the six corners of the hexagon is a cluster of three vessels: very small branches of the hepatic artery, the portal vein, and a small bile duct. The artery and vein feed their blood into the sinusoids, where it flows slowly to the hub. The hub is called the central vein and is a very small branch of the hepatic vein. It collects the blood for return to the hepatic vein and then to the heart. The spokes form the walls of the sinusoids and are made up of hepatocytes (liver cells), which

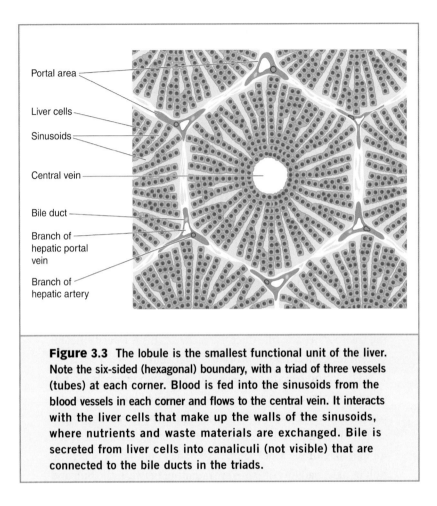

Portal area

Liver cells

Sinusoids

Central vein

Bile duct

Branch of
hepatic portal
vein

Branch of
hepatic artery

Figure 3.3 The lobule is the smallest functional unit of the liver. Note the six-sided (hexagonal) boundary, with a triad of three vessels (tubes) at each corner. Blood is fed into the sinusoids from the blood vessels in each corner and flows to the central vein. It interacts with the liver cells that make up the walls of the sinusoids, where nutrients and waste materials are exchanged. Bile is secreted from liver cells into canaliculi (not visible) that are connected to the bile ducts in the triads.

are the cells that do all the work of the liver. Their work consists of taking up materials from the blood, modifying these materials, and delivering the modified and new materials back to the blood and into the bile ducts. The bile ducts are not connected directly to the blood. They receive bile from the canaliculi between the hepatocytes, which produce and excrete bile into them. It is the hepatocytes that become infected by the hepatitis viruses.

Liver specialists recognize that the liver performs more than 500 important functions. This organ is truly a chemical factory; an energy, vitamin, and mineral storage reservoir; a waste treatment plant; and a regulator of other organs. Here are some of its major functions: The liver produces most of the important proteins that are needed in blood. It produces special proteins that carry fats throughout our body. It takes up sugars from the blood and converts them into a special form (glycogen) for storage, and it breaks down the glycogen and releases sugar in the form of glucose to the blood when energy is needed by other parts of the body. It takes up from or releases to the blood amino acids as needed and regulates the blood levels of these protein building blocks. It helps to process hemoglobin (a protein-iron compound found in the blood) from dying red blood cells by saving iron for reuse and forming modified bilirubin for release to the bile (see Chapter 2). It converts ammonia, which is toxic and is released when proteins are broken down, to less toxic urea, which is returned to the blood and excreted in the urine. It produces chemicals that are essential for blood clotting (called **coagulation**) or clotting factors, and it makes bile salts for release to the bile, which are essential for the normal digestion of fats in the small intestine. The liver helps fight infections by removing and destroying bacteria from our blood and by secreting some immune factors that help the cells of the immune system fight infections. Finally, the liver removes foreign and toxic substances from the blood, including therapeutic drugs, and destroys them. Broken-down fragments of wastes and toxic substances are modified and released to the bile for ultimate disposal in the feces and to the blood where they are filtered by the kidneys for disposal in the urine.

Viral hepatitis is a serious illness because the hepatitis viruses invade the hepatocytes and interfere with their normal functions. Consequently, the liver cannot do a proper job of supporting the rest of the body. Another serious consequence of viral infection is that the immune system begins attacking and destroying the infected hepatocytes. If this goes on for less

BILE

Bile is a dark yellow-green, bitter, alkaline fluid secreted by liver cells into the bile ducts. It is made up of waste products, cholesterol, and bile salts. Bile drains waste from the liver into the gut for excretion in the feces. This is an extremely important mechanism for eliminating waste and toxic substances from the body. Bile salts aid in the breakdown of dietary fats in the small intestine, in the absorption of these fats into the blood, and in the transport of fat to the liver for further processing. The bile salts are recovered by the liver and recycled. Fats, especially the compounds called fatty acids, are important parts of cell structures, some hormones, chemicals used for regulation of blood pressure and the immune response, and cell metabolism. Although the body can make many fats from other chemicals, including sugars, it is more efficient to acquire them in the diet. Some fatty acids cannot be made by the human body and are called essential fatty acids because they are necessary for normal health. We must acquire these in the diet. Two examples are linoleic acid (an omega-6 fatty acid) and alpha-linolenic acid (an omega-3 fatty acid). These compounds are involved in the production of energy by cells; the exchange of oxygen between the lungs and the blood; the synthesis of hemoglobin, which is the oxygen-carrying protein in red blood cells; the regulation of cell growth and division; and nerve function.

Fats do not dissolve in water. This is a major problem when we consider how fats might be moved from the gut across the intestinal wall into the blood and be transported by the blood throughout the body, especially to the liver. The bile salts emulsify (break up or dissolve) the fats. That is, one part of the bile salt molecule binds to or dissolves in the fat and the other part dissolves in water. A very small fat droplet is surrounded by many bile salts, with part of each salt molecule dissolved in the fat and the other part dissolved in the water. One of the most important fat-binding proteins, and also the most abundant protein in blood plasma, is albumin. Albumin serves many functions in blood, including the binding and transport of fatty acids.

than 6 months, before the virus is eliminated, then the damaged liver will regenerate and there will be no long-term damage. However, some viruses cannot be eliminated completely by the immune system. Remember that up to 75% of liver cells can be lost before there is a serious loss of liver function. It may take 20 or more years for this level of liver destruction to develop, and the infected person may not know he or she is sick until liver failure starts.

We will next review the process of inflammation and the details of the immune system that are important for under-standing hepatitis.

4

Inflammation and the Immune Response

Hepatitis means "inflammation of the liver." Just what is inflammation? Inflammation is a set of complex cellular and chemical reactions in blood vessels and the surrounding tissues in response to injury or to abnormal stimulation caused by chemical (such as alcohol in the liver or bee venom in the skin) or biologic agents (such as bacteria and viruses). Characteristic signs of inflammation are redness, higher-than-normal tissue warmth or heat, swelling, and pain. These signs are localized to the area of injury or infection and are most readily noted when the inflammation is on the body surface. Not all of these signs are present in every person with inflammation. In addition, a person with a major inflammation may develop a fever as well as malaise, anorexia (appetite loss), and nausea. For example, tuberculosis causes major inflammation of the lung and other tissues. Victims become anorexic and lose a lot of weight, which is why the disease has also been called "consumption." Figure 4.1 shows an example of the cut surfaces of a normal liver.

INFLAMMATION AND HEALING

Inflammation in response to infection begins when white blood cells recognize an invading virus or bacterium and release chemicals that alert other immune system cells that an invader is present. Then, a very complicated cascade of events follows. Blood flow increases to the site of infection. This allows more immune cells to reach the site to fight the infection, and the blood delivers more nutrients and oxygen to the tissue

34

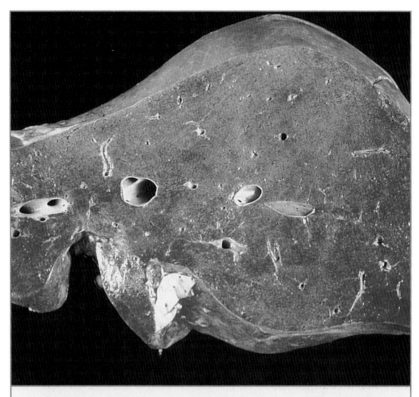

Figure 4.1 Shown here is a cross-section of a healthy liver made with a sharp knife. This is how the liver would appear without the aid of magnification. Some large blood vessels can be seen. Note the fine texture of the red-brown liver tissue.

cells to provide for increased metabolism and oxygen burning. One result of this is that the tissue becomes warmer or heats up. The blood vessels leak water, white blood cells, and proteins. This causes swelling and gives white blood cells and immune system proteins easier access to infected sites to attack the invader in the tissues. Meanwhile, the inflammatory chemicals irritate nerve endings in the tissue, which causes pain.

Healing of tissue damage during inflammation proceeds through three processes, and healing begins almost as soon as inflammation begins. The healing actually competes with the inflammation. If the cause of inflammation cannot be removed, then the healing processes may produce abnormal or nonfunctional tissues. This is often the case in chronic hepatitis when cirrhosis develops.

The resolution process of healing occurs early when there is little tissue damage. Specialized cells called **macrophages** enter the inflamed area from the blood and scavenge (eat) dead cells and any other debris created by the injury or infection, such as pus. The original structure of the tissue is left intact. If the immune system defeats the invading microbe, the tissue is restored to normal.

The regeneration process of healing occurs when lost cells are replaced by **proliferation** (division and growth) of cells of the same kind. Liver hepatocytes are most capable of this response, although other tissues like skin and bones have a limited ability to regenerate small losses. The key to a successful regeneration is to accurately reproduce the structure of the damaged tissue. This is easy with a simple tissue like the skin, but it is very difficult for a complex organ like the liver. Imperfect regeneration may occur in the liver because only the hepatocytes proliferate easily. Other cells that contribute to the structure of the liver do not reproduce as well.

Extensive or ongoing damage to the liver structure can result in cirrhosis, a condition of abnormal tissue structure and abnormal function. Hepatocytes proliferate but cannot assemble into the normal lobular structure. Instead, they form small balls or nodules that are isolated from the blood because new blood vessels do not develop normally and scarring obstructs them. An example of a liver with severe cirrhosis is shown in Figure 4.2. Ongoing liver damage can occur with chronic infections, including some forms of viral hepatitis (Figure 4.3), or with chronic exposure to toxic chemicals such as alcohol. Cirrhosis is not reversible, but its progress can be stopped in some cases. However, it ultimately causes death if it proceeds for very long.

Figure 4.2 This is a cross-section made with a sharp knife of a liver with advanced cirrhosis. The image has been magnified about 3 times. Some large blood vessels can be seen. Obstructed blood flow due to scarring occurs at the level of the capillaries and lobules, which are not visible in this view. Note the metric scale (graduated in centimeters) at the lower right. Compare the coarse texture of this tissue with the normal texture of the liver in Figure 4.1 on page 35. Note the many balls, or nodules, which are about 3 to 5 mm in diameter, that have a yellow color where liver cells have proliferated abnormally around scar tissue. Often the nodules will fuse to form larger nodules up to 5 cm in diameter. The nodules have a very poor blood supply and most of this tissue is not functional.

The repair process of healing results in the formation of scars. Fibroblasts are specialized cells present in all tissues that produce the structural network or meshwork of fibers in a tissue that connects or holds all the other cells together. This network is called connective tissue and consists of many different proteins, including the most abundant one, collagen. When extensive tissue loss has happened and regeneration is slow or not occurring at all, fibroblasts migrate to the damaged

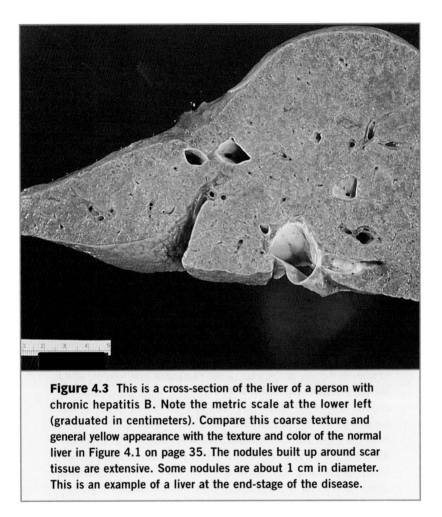

Figure 4.3 This is a cross-section of the liver of a person with chronic hepatitis B. Note the metric scale at the lower left (graduated in centimeters). Compare this coarse texture and general yellow appearance with the texture and color of the normal liver in Figure 4.1 on page 35. The nodules built up around scar tissue are extensive. Some nodules are about 1 cm in diameter. This is an example of a liver at the end-stage of the disease.

area and produce collagen to fill the void. The collagen ultimately becomes a scar.

IMMUNE RESPONSE

The immune response has humoral (pertaining to body fluids) and cellular parts. The **humoral response** involves antibodies that are produced by a special class of white blood cells called B lymphocytes. Antibodies are also called **immunoglobulins**, abbreviated Ig. They are proteins that interact specifically with a foreign substance or antigen. They actually react with a small part of the antigen called an **epitope**. The antibodies are released by the **B cells** and circulate in the blood separately or bound to the surface of white blood cells. There are five classes of immunoglobulins: IgG, IgM, IgA, IgD, and IgE. IgG and IgM make up 93% of the antibodies found in our blood. IgM antibodies are usually the first to be produced in response to an antigen, followed by the IgG antibodies, which usually remain in the blood after an infection is over and provide immunity against reinfection.

Antibodies are Y-shaped proteins produced by B cells. Antigens are proteins with small structural parts called epitopes that are unique to the foreign invader. The B cell modifies part of the basic antibody protein to a structure that is complementary to the antigen epitope so that parts of the antigen and antibody can fit together like a lock and key (Figure 4.4).

Antibodies work in one of three specific ways. In the first, they may bind to the antigens on the surface of a bacterium or virus and make that invader recognizable by a special class of cells called **phagocytes** that then engulf and destroy the invader through a process called **phagocytosis**. A second kind of antibody binds to the antigens on the surface of a virus and prevents the virus from entering cells. This blocks the infection because viruses must enter cells to reproduce. Viruses do not have reproductive machinery of their own and must "hijack" the reproductive machinery of the cells they infect. After binding to antigen, the third kind of antibodies then react with substances produced by the liver called **complement proteins**. This interaction results in the opening up of the cell membrane of the bacterium or the infected cell and the destruction of the target by an explosion-like process known as **lysis**. Macrophages then clean up the mess.

The cellular response involves another special class of white blood cells, called **T lymphocytes** because the cells originate in the thymus gland, which is a small gland located high in

(continued on page 41)

KILLER T CELLS AND APOPTOSIS

Killer T cells, also known as cytotoxic T cells, are activated by helper T cells that give them a modified copy of an antigen's epitope. An infected cell may succeed in getting a copy of an epitope from the microbe once it is inside the cell. The cell can then attach this epitope to the external surface of its own cell membrane, where an activated killer T cell can recognize and bind to it. Once binding occurs, a series of changes is triggered in the T cell, causing a specific kind of attack on the infected cell that leads to the death of the cell by **apoptosis** (a pattern of cell death). It can be said that the T cell induces the suicide of the target cell because all destructive effects are produced by the target cell itself. Cell death by apoptosis is also known as programmed cell death because it occurs in an orderly, well-defined manner. Apoptosis can be triggered in many ways and also serves to eliminate old and defective cells when there is no infection.

During apoptosis, a cascade of chemical reactions begins in the infected cell, which leads to the activation of a group of enzymes known as caspases. Some caspases destroy proteins that make up the structural skeleton of the cell, others destroy proteins in the cell nucleus that are essential for gene function, and others activate enzymes that destroy the cell's DNA. Some caspases can also destroy the DNA or RNA of an infecting microbe, thus killing it within the cell. These destructive events do not cause the cell to just disintegrate and release all of its contents to the surrounding tissue, as in the process known as lysis. With apoptosis, the cell ultimately breaks up into fragments that enclose cell contents, including the infecting agent. These fragments are then taken up by macrophages that devour and destroy them completely. The killer T cells are not destroyed in this process. After they have initiated apoptosis in one cell, they can detach and look for other infected cells.

After the killer T cells have done their job and all of the infecting agent has been destroyed, the immune response must be terminated, or else the T cells will begin to attack healthy cells. Termination occurs when the T cells bind to each other and, for lack of a better target, initiate apoptosis in each other.

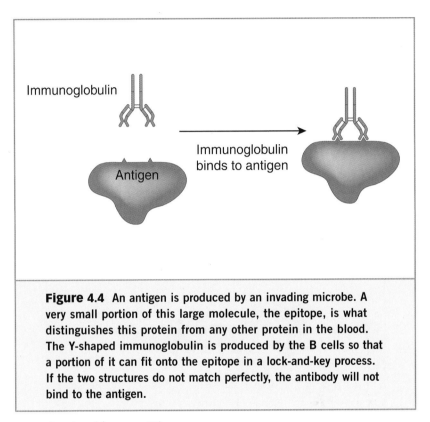

Figure 4.4 An antigen is produced by an invading microbe. A very small portion of this large molecule, the epitope, is what distinguishes this protein from any other protein in the blood. The Y-shaped immunoglobulin is produced by the B cells so that a portion of it can fit onto the epitope in a lock-and-key process. If the two structures do not match perfectly, the antibody will not bind to the antigen.

(continued from page 39)

the chest behind the breastbone. There are two kinds of T cells: **helper T cells** and **killer T cells**. Helper T cells are the guardians or patrolmen of the body. They are the first to recognize an antigen. Next, they alert the B cells (see Figure 4.5) and give them the epitope template to make specific antibodies against the invader. They then coordinate the overall immune response. Helper T cells also activate the killer T cells and give them a processed copy of the antigen epitope. The killer T cells are the enforcers. They use the epitope information to identify, attack, and destroy diseased cells. Infected cells can take an epitope from the invading microbe and attach it to the cell surface, where activated killer T cells can recognize it. The epitope attachment occurs by way of a cell membrane protein known

Figure 4.5 The cellular immune response to a virus is illustrated here. An infected cell (left) has successfully put a viral epitope (red triangle) onto a major histocompatibility complex (MHC) on its surface. A killer T cell (right), also known as a CD8+ cytotoxic T cell, has been activated and given a complementary copy of the epitope to recognize and bind to it at the MHC. Binding triggers apoptosis in the infected cell, destroying its internal structure and breaking it up into many dense, membrane-enclosed particles that also contain the viruses. The killer T cell is not affected, and is free to attack other infected cells.

as a **major histocompatibility complex** (**MHC**). Killer T cells attack the diseased cells, not the foreign body, and are very important for fighting viral infections. Destruction of an infected cell also eliminates the viruses in that cell. Both B and T lymphocytes circulate within the blood, on guard for foreign invaders, but they must be activated by the helper T cells to do their job.

When a person is initially infected with a hepatitis virus, the immune system attempts to respond and eliminate the virus—a typical response to any virus or other microbe. But the immune system also has special features that depend on the nature of the virus. Next, we will review viruses, how they work, why they cause trouble, and how health professionals test for them.

5

The Story of Viruses

To understand the discussions about the specific hepatitis viruses in the chapters that follow, some important background information about viruses is needed.

Viruses are among the smallest biological things we know of. At one time, viruses were considered the smallest, but a smaller group of infectious objects called prions has been found. (Little is known about prions at this time). The picornaviruses are among the smallest viruses and measure 25 to 35 nanometers in diameter. This is extremely small. One nanometer is about 40 billionths of an inch. This family of very small viruses includes those that cause poliomyelitis, the common cold, and hepatitis A. Viruses are 10 to 100 times smaller than bacteria and up to 100,000 times smaller than the head of a pin. They are not visible with a standard light microscope, but can be viewed with an electron microscope. Electron microscopes can magnify objects by up to 1 million times their size, or about 200 times more than the best light microscopes. The first image of a virus was obtained only after the electron microscope was developed in the 1930s.

More than 400 different viruses are known that infect humans. Viruses have existed about as long as life itself, although they probably could not develop before the very first cells did because they need cells to reproduce.

VIRAL REPLICATION

Viruses replicate (reproduce) in five steps: (1) The virus attaches to a host cell; (2) it penetrates the host; (3) viral nucleic acid is released into the host, where it initiates and guides the production or synthesis of new viral protein and nucleic acid using the machinery of the host cell; (4) new viruses, made up of newly synthesized viral nucleic acid and proteins, are assembled with the help of other proteins that are coded by viral nucleic acid and synthesized by the infected cell; and (5) the new viruses leave the host to search for new hosts. Viruses are pure parasites. They cannot live independently. They are able to reproduce and function only inside a host cell, and they use the energy normally available to the host for its own functions to reproduce. Each virus has unique details for its replication (see Figure 5.1), but all conform to this general format. We will describe the replication process for each hepatitis virus later.

An active virus essentially hijacks the host cell's metabolic machinery for its own purposes. The metabolic machinery of a cell is composed of all the vital chemical reactions that are required to keep the cell alive and to perform its special functions. The consequence of this hijacking is that the host cell is less able to meet its own needs or the needs of other cells in the body that depend on it. Cells may die and the whole organism may develop symptoms that are caused by the loss of important cell functions. An infected person feels sick for these reasons and because the immune response to the virus can cause symptoms such as inflammation and fever.

Viruses have relatively simple structures. They consist of a **nucleic acid**, which can be either **DNA** or **RNA**, and one or a few proteins. One criterion for classifying viruses is whether they have DNA or RNA. Viral nucleic acid usually has only a few genes, perhaps 20 or fewer, which are needed to ensure the reproduction of the virus. The nucleic acid may be a single strand or a double strand. How many strands it has is another way to classify viruses.

The nucleic acid in a virus is enclosed by a protein coat known as a **capsid**, which helps protect the nucleic acid from attack by enzymes. It contains special sites that allow it to recognize and attach to a host cell and other sites that allow it

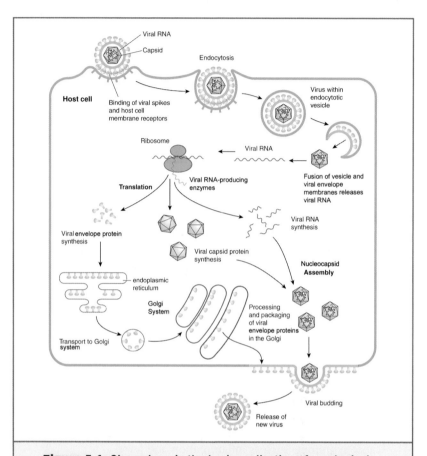

Figure 5.1 Shown here is the basic replication of a spherical virus with an envelope. Viral spikes recognize binding sites on a host cell and help the virus attach to the cell membrane. This causes the cell membrane to wrap around the virus and pinch off into the **cytoplasm** (the substance inside a cell) in a process known as endocytosis. The viral envelope then fuses with the endocytotic vesicle membrane, causing the release of capsids into the cytoplasm. Viral RNA is liberated, leading to activation of viral protein synthesis by the cell's ribosomes and production of more viral RNA. The new materials are assembled and packaged by the cell structures shown and new viruses are released by **budding**. This is one way by which viruses penetrate cells and are released; the process in the cytoplasm that is described is essentially the same for all viruses.

to penetrate the host cell membrane and enter the cell. Many viruses have spikes of protein that make the capsid look like a pincushion. These spikes extend out from the capsid surface and contain the host-recognition sites that allow the virus to bind to the surface of a host cell. Remarkably, the capsids of

DNA AND THE GENETIC CODE

There are two kinds of nucleic acid that are named for the molecular subunits or building blocks that make up their backbones. The building block deoxyribose, which is a kind of sugar molecule, makes up deoxyribonucleic acid, or DNA. DNA is always present in the cell nucleus in animals and contains all the genes that define what an animal is. It is a huge molecule that is usually twisted into a helix like a screw. In animals, two strands of the helix are twisted together into a double helix that looks rather like two strings of beads that have been twisted together.

Attached to each deoxyribose is one of four molecules. Two of these molecules are called purines, named adenine (A) and guanine (G). The other two molecules are called pyrimidines and named thymine (T) and cytosine (C). These molecules have a chemical property that classifies them as bases. They also like to link up loosely with each other to form base pairs in a very specific manner. They never link up with the other bases. Thus, we get the pairs A–T and C–G, and no others. When an adenine on one DNA strand is opposite a thymine on the other strand, the two link up. The same thing happens between cytosine and guanine. In fact, the two strands are synthesized to be complementary so that opposite bases always link up. The sequence of bases in one strand of the DNA defines the genetic code. A set of three successive bases is called a codon and defines a single amino acid. For example, the codon TTC defines the amino acid phenylalanine and the codon ACG defines the amino acid threonine.

some viruses consist of a single kind of protein. Other capsids have 10 different proteins. The capsid is made up of many protein subunits called **capsomers**. About 150 to 200 capsomers are assembled into the final capsid structure around the nucleic acid during reproduction of the virus.

The capsid-enclosed nucleic acid is called a **nucleocapsid**. Sometimes the nucleocapsid makes up the complete virus. The shape of the capsid depends on the general shape of the nucleic acid. If the nucleic acid is like an extended, thick, twisted string or rope, it will form a screw-like structure called a helix. The capsomers assemble around this extended string to form a cylinder or rod-shaped nucleocapsid. Viruses with this structure are referred to as helical viruses (Figure 5.2)

RNA AND PROTEIN SYNTHESIS

The building block ribose, another sugar molecule that is similar to but different from deoxyribose, makes up ribonucleic acid, or RNA. RNA occurs in three important and different forms. All forms of RNA are produced in the cell nucleus but move out into the cytoplasm, where they perform their functions. Messenger RNA (mRNA) contains all the codons in the proper sequence needed to produce a single protein from the amino acid building blocks of proteins. It acquires this information from the gene for the protein in a process called **transcription**. mRNA is also a large molecule, though not as large as DNA. The larger the protein to be built, the larger the mRNA. mRNA is moved from the nucleus into the cytoplasm, where protein synthesis occurs.

Within the cytoplasm is a second form of RNA known as transfer RNA, or tRNA. It is much smaller than mRNA and has a special function. There is one kind of tRNA for each of the 20 different amino acids that can be in a protein. Each tRNA recognizes one amino acid and can because of the helical twist of the nucleic acid, and the nucleic acid is usually single-stranded RNA—probably the simplest form of a virus. If the nucleic acid string is balled up rather than extended, then the capsid forms a 20-sided polygon to enclose the ball, called an icosahedron, whose sides are equilateral triangles. The icosahedron looks like a sphere because it has so many sides, and this form of nucleocapsid is often called spherical (Figure 5.3). Another criterion for classifying a virus is its helical or spherical structure. Spherical viruses are the most common, and all hepatitis viruses are spherical.

A single capsomer protein may perform multiple functions for the virus because it is usually very large and can have many functional zones along its length. The nucleocapsid of

grab onto or bind it. The tRNA serves to transfer the amino acid from the cytoplasm into the protein-synthesizing complex known as the ribosome.

The third form of RNA is ribosomal RNA (rRNA). It is coiled up and is a crucial part of the ribosome. Ribosomes are attached to the surface of membrane-enclosed sacks called the endoplasmic reticulum, or ER. mRNA binds to a ribosome and the rRNA interprets the codon sequence in the mRNA for making a protein. The tRNA binds to the rRNA to deliver the specific amino acid called for by a codon on the mRNA. The mRNA slides through the rRNA from one end to the other. At each codon, a tRNA delivers the amino acid called for and detaches from the ribosome, the amino acid is incorporated into the growing protein molecule, and the rRNA shifts to read another codon. The newly synthesized protein may be released into the cell cytoplasm or into the interior of the ER, where it may undergo additional changes before it is released to the cytoplasm as a fully functional protein.

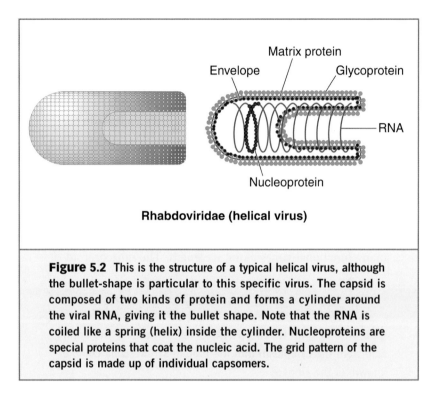

Rhabdoviridae (helical virus)

Figure 5.2 This is the structure of a typical helical virus, although the bullet-shape is particular to this specific virus. The capsid is composed of two kinds of protein and forms a cylinder around the viral RNA, giving it the bullet shape. Note that the RNA is coiled like a spring (helix) inside the cylinder. Nucleoproteins are special proteins that coat the nucleic acid. The grid pattern of the capsid is made up of individual capsomers.

some viruses is enclosed by a membrane called the envelope. This membrane is derived from the host cell membrane as the virus exits the host cell in a process called budding. Budding occurs when a virus pushes outward on the cell membrane and the membrane folds around the capsid until finally the membrane breaks free of the cell and closes up with the virus inside (recall Figure 5.1). However, the virus always inserts some of its own proteins from the capsid into the envelope. These serve to attach and bind the virus to other host cells, which are like the spike proteins described above. The presence or absence of an envelope is yet another criterion for classifying a virus. Budding does not necessarily kill the host.

Not all viruses exit the host cell by budding. Others release enzymes that bore holes in the cell membrane that cause the membrane to rupture, or lyse, thereby liberating the virus in the

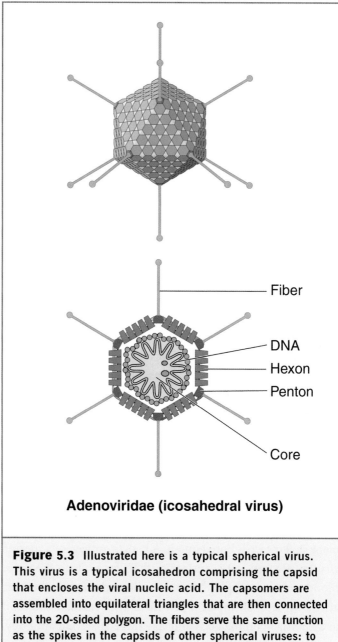

Fiber

DNA

Hexon

Penton

Core

Adenoviridae (icosahedral virus)

Figure 5.3 Illustrated here is a typical spherical virus. This virus is a typical icosahedron comprising the capsid that encloses the viral nucleic acid. The capsomers are assembled into equilateral triangles that are then connected into the 20-sided polygon. The fibers serve the same function as the spikes in the capsids of other spherical viruses: to recognize and bind to receptors on a host cell.

form of a nucleocapsid. The complete virus structure that exits a host cell and can infect other cells is referred to as a **virion**.

TESTING FOR VIRUSES

Testing for a virus can be done by several methods. The following are those used routinely by medical laboratories for detection of the hepatitis viruses.

Radioimmunoassay and Immunofluorescence

A blood sample is treated with an antibody that is labeled with a radioactive material in a radioimmunoassay (RIA), or with a molecule that glows when a light shines on it, in an immunofluorescence assay. If an antigen is present, the antibody binds to it and the complex can be detected by sensitive measuring techniques.

ELISA

A second method of establishing that a virus infection is present is the detection of specific antibodies in the blood (see Chapter 4). This approach cannot establish that there is still live virus because the immune system ensures that some antibody is always present even after a virus has been successfully eliminated. This is an important and key function of the immune system in providing immunity to reinfection by the same microbe. Furthermore, the immune system may not yet have produced antibody at the time of the test.

An enzyme-linked immunosorbent assay (ELISA) is used most frequently (Figure 5.4). A glass plate is prepared that has many shallow wells bored into it. A known antigen of a specific virus is attached to the surface of the glass walls in the wells. Blood serum is applied to the wells and then washed off after a while. If antibody is present in the serum, it will bind to the antigen on the glass and stay there. A second antibody, prepared in the laboratory and known to bind to all human antibodies, is then applied to the well. If viral antibody is

Figure 5.4 An ELISA is a procedure used to identify viruses. The glass plate used for this test has 96 wells. Each well may be coated with one antigen specific for the virus the doctors are looking for, or groups of wells may each have a different antigen. Patient serum is added to each well, and the procedure occurs as shown. If a specific antibody is present in serum, it will cause a color change in the wells that contain the correct antigen.

present, the secondary antibody will bind to it. The secondary antibody has an enzyme attached (linked) to it that can react with certain chemicals called chromogens and change their colors. The secondary antibody is washed off after a while and a chromogen solution is applied. Finally, the well is inspected for color to determine whether an antibody has been found. The intensity of the color is related directly to the amount of antibody in the sample, so it is also possible to measure the concentration of antibody in the blood.

A simple ELISA test may not be sensitive enough to detect some viruses, such as the hepatitis C virus. A second-generation enzyme immunoassay, EIA-2, was developed in 1992. It is much more sensitive than ELISA and has enabled routine screening of donated blood for hepatitis C virus. This test is done much like an ELISA, except that several viral antigens are used rather than just one antigen. The EIA-2 test can give false-positive results, however.

Another test, called a recombinant immunoblot assay, was developed to check for false-positive results with the EIA-2 or RIBA-2. The term *recombinant* refers to the technique used to manufacture four antigens that are known to be present in the virus. In this test, these antigens are attached to a strip of special paper and a sample of blood serum is blotted onto the strip. If antibodies are present, they bind to the antigens on the strip and cause a color change. The RIBA-2 test is used routinely in blood screening whenever the EIA-2 test is positive for hepatitis C virus. If both tests are positive, it is concluded that hepatitis C virus antigens are in the sample. If the EIA-2 test is positive and the RIBA-2 test is negative, a false-positive test result has probably occurred. A second blood sample and retesting may be done.

PCR

A third method of virus detection is to measure the viral nucleic acid extracted from the blood. The polymerase chain reaction (PCR) makes this possible. PCR is a very sensitive method and is useful only when the infection is active and live virus is present in the blood. PCR is a chemical reaction produced by a polymerase enzyme that replicates the viral nucleic acid as long as there are bases or nucleic acid building blocks available. Building blocks and enzymes are added to a serum sample. A reaction starts if there is any nucleic acid present at all and it just keeps going until all building blocks are used up. However, PCR is expensive to perform and is not used as routinely as other methods. Furthermore, medical scientists have not agreed upon standards for doing the test and the Food and Drug Administration (FDA) has approved it only for screening for active infections of some viruses, such as hepatitis C virus.

6

Hepatitis A

RHONDA

Rhonda was a high school senior who enjoyed eating fresh fruits and vegetables. One day she went out for lunch with some friends to a popular restaurant known for its all-you-can-eat salad bar. Rhonda took advantage of the salad bar and impressed her friends with how much salad she could eat. Everyone had a good time, and Rhonda's reputation was sealed as the premier salad-cruncher in town.

Three weeks after the lunch party, Rhonda became ill. First, she felt very tired and had a mild fever. It wasn't flu season, but she thought she might have picked up some kind of bug. She rested for a day but did not get better. In fact, she became nauseated, had pain in her abdomen, and began to vomit. Her mother made an appointment for her to see the doctor the next day. On the day of her appointment, Rhonda noticed that her urine had turned very dark yellow. The doctor examined Rhonda and decided to do a blood test to screen for microbe infections. He suspected viral hepatitis because Rhonda's symptoms were a textbook example of the acute hepatitis symptoms discussed in Chapter 2. He also knew from her medical history that Rhonda had not been vaccinated for hepatitis A or B. He advised Rhonda to rest at home and be patient while he waited for the test results.

The next day, the whites of Rhonda's eyes yellowed. She had jaundice; she was in the icteric phase of a hepatitis infection (see Chapter 2). Her fever and other symptoms, except fatigue, were not as bad. She actually began to feel better, but still had jaundice and was fatigued. The doctor called a day later and said that Rhonda's test result for hepatitis A was positive. In other words, her blood level of the antibody for the

56

hepatitis A virus, IgM-A, was high (see Chapter 4). This was a good sign because it meant her immune system was fighting the infection and would ultimately eliminate the virus. She was told that her symptoms should subside within a few weeks and that she should recover completely in a month or two. The jaundice might get worse for the next week or so, but then would clear up as she recovered. She would have to avoid strenuous activity and get plenty of rest, but she could resume most of her activities as soon as she felt well enough. She would then be immune to future hepatitis A infections for the rest of her life.

The doctor also advised Rhonda and her family not to share eating utensils or drinking glasses. Rhonda must wash her hands frequently, especially after a bowel movement, and should not help with food preparation or dishwashing until after she was fully recovered. Rhonda was delighted with that last piece of advice! The doctor wanted Rhonda to make weekly office visits until she had recovered so he could track the progress of the disease. There was a very slight chance that the infection could trigger fulminant hepatitis (see Chapter 2), and the doctor wanted to be on the lookout for it.

The source of Rhonda's infection was a mystery to everyone. The doctor reported Rhonda's infection to the public health authorities. This is a routine procedure for all hepatitis infections and certain other communicable diseases. Public health authorities do not need to know the names of patients, but they need to know about communicable infections to determine whether a disease **outbreak** (sudden increase of a disease in a small area) is in progress. Such knowledge enables them to take steps to curb the outbreak and protect the public health. The authorities observed that within the past month, they had received reports of 110 hepatitis A infections in the county where Rhonda lives. Two of the people, who were elderly, died from fulminant hepatitis. All of the surviving victims recovered fully. The health officials noted that four of the infected people worked as waitresses in the same restaurant that Rhonda had visited. A little more investigation revealed that all of the victims had eaten there. This was considered an outbreak. Health inspectors visited the restaurant and encouraged the employees to have blood tests. The restaurant closed until further notice. One restaurant employee, a dishwasher, was found to have had a hepatitis A infection, although he had not suffered any symptoms. The restaurant did a thorough cleaning of the kitchen and all of its dishes, silverware, and cooking utensils with a strong bleach solution before it reopened.

HEPATITIS A VIRUS

Hepatitis A virus, abbreviated HAV, is among the smallest of viruses. It belongs to the family of picornaviruses, which includes the poliovirus and the rhinoviruses that cause the common cold. The virus has an icosahedron (20-sided)-shaped capsid. The capsid is made up of 60 capsomers, which are composed of 4 different proteins. Three of the proteins are exposed on the surface of the capsid and contain the binding sites that allow the virus to attach to and enter a host cell. The nucleic acid is single-stranded RNA. It has is no envelope (see Chapter 5).

The most important immune response (Chapter 4) to HAV is cellular rather than **humoral** (pertaining to body fluids). Killer T cells are activated that attack and destroy infected hepatocytes by inducing apoptosis (programmed cell death). In most cases, the process does not go on long enough to cause major damage to the liver, and hepatocytes regenerate once the virus is gone. B cells, activated by the helper T cells, help activate the killer T cells and produce the immunoglobulin IgM-A. There is a significant amount of virus in the blood during the acute phase of the infection, and IgM-A attacks that virus directly. However, most of the virus is found inside the hepatocytes or shed in the feces. IgM-A serves as an important marker for an acute HAV infection and is looked for in blood tests. Its level in the blood reaches a peak about 6 weeks after infection and then fades away. However, a second antibody, IgG-A, is produced more slowly by the B cells. This antibody reaches a high level in the blood 2 months after infection and remains there for a very long time. It is IgG-A that can provide a defense against future infections by HAV by attacking the virus directly as it enters the blood and before it can enter the hepatocytes. IgG-A in the blood with no IgM-A is proof that a person has been immunized against hepatitis A, either through a self-limited infection (as with the dishwasher at the restaurant) or a vaccine.

The virus reproduces in the general way described in Chapter 5. Once the virus enters the cell, it releases its nucleic acid into the cytoplasm. The viral RNA takes control of the cell's nucleic acid and protein synthesis systems to produce more viral RNA and capsid proteins (Figure 6.1). Capsomers assemble into capsids that enclose a single viral RNA. The capsids are then enclosed within a small membranous vesicle (like a bubble) that can fuse with the hepatocyte membrane only at sites next to bile canaliculi. The vesicles fuse, open up to the outside, and release virus to the bile. This process does not kill the hepatocytes; rather, it is the killer T cells that do so. Once in the bile, the new viruses can infect neighboring hepatocytes or make their way to the gut, where some reenter the blood and the rest are shed in the feces.

TRANSMISSION OF HAV

People with active virus infections are called **carriers** (people who are infected but are symptom-free). Trillions of viruses are present in a carrier. A person may acquire an HAV infection by contact with infected feces or with objects that have come in contact with infected feces, followed by ingestion of the virus. Only 10 to 100 viruses need to be ingested to establish an infection.

HAV is an enteric virus. The ingested virus crosses the gut wall, enters the blood, finds its way to the liver, and infects

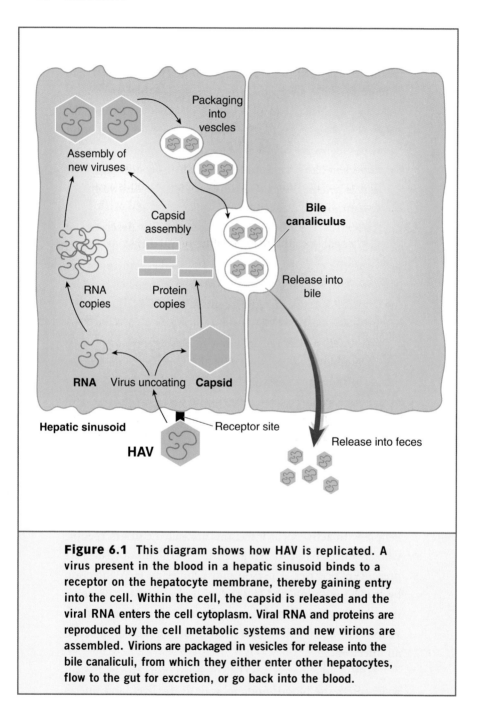

Figure 6.1 This diagram shows how HAV is replicated. A virus present in the blood in a hepatic sinusoid binds to a receptor on the hepatocyte membrane, thereby gaining entry into the cell. Within the cell, the capsid is released and the viral RNA enters the cell cytoplasm. Viral RNA and proteins are reproduced by the cell metabolic systems and new virions are assembled. Virions are packaged in vesicles for release into the bile canaliculi, from which they either enter other hepatocytes, flow to the gut for excretion, or go back into the blood.

hepatocytes. Feces-contaminated water is the principal route of transmission of HAV. Carriers who are careless about handwashing may pass the virus on to others. Other ways of acquiring an infection include eating fresh foods that have been handled by a carrier or washed with contaminated water; using eating utensils that have been handled by a carrier; changing the diaper of an infected infant or touching a diaper-changing table that has not been well cleaned; sharing eating utensils or food handled by a family member who is a carrier; eating raw shellfish harvested from or washed with contaminated water; and having sexual relations with a carrier, especially anal sex. Rhonda probably ingested HAV by eating with contaminated utensils in the restaurant.

The older a person is, the more likely it is that HAV will cause symptoms. Infants and young children rarely suffer symptoms, so parents have no way of knowing that a child is ill. Symptom-free carriers are likely to spread the disease. An estimated 90% of children in underdeveloped countries are infected early in life and do not suffer symptoms; therefore, most adults who were born and raised in such countries are immune to the disease. However, visitors from developed countries are at a very high risk for infection unless they have been immunized.

WHERE THE DISEASE OCCURS

Hepatitis A is a very serious disease worldwide. About 1.5 million cases are reported to the World Health Organization (WHO) every year. These cases cost an estimated $3 billion per year. About 35,000 of these cases arise in the United States, costing about $500 million per year. Experts estimate that 15 million new cases actually arise each year. The disease is misdiagnosed and underreported, probably because it often is symptom-free or causes minor flu-like symptoms, and because it is strictly an acute disease with a short duration. The **incidence** (number of new cases per year among a specified number of people) of the disease is very high in most underdeveloped countries with poor sanitation, water, and public health systems.

PREVENTION OF HAV

Good personal hygiene is one of the best ways to avoid HAV infection (Figure 6.2), as is being careful about the water you drink. Public health measures to protect the water supply can

PUBLIC HEALTH AND CONSEQUENCES OF THE DISEASE

You may wonder why hepatitis A is considered a serious health problem in view of its mild or absent symptoms. Adults are more likely to suffer symptoms that are severe enough to prevent them from working for a few weeks or months, and adults older than 50 can be disabled for months or become seriously ill because of complications from other medical problems. Lost work in a developed country is usually a minor inconvenience because most people are protected by employer-provided sick leave. Lost work in an underdeveloped country can be very serious, however. Poor people have limited opportunities for work. Subsistence farmers could lose a harvest and an entire family could face starvation.

The high incidence of hepatitis A in underdeveloped countries is important for public health in the United States, Europe, and Japan. Many foodstuffs, especially fresh fruits and vegetables, are imported from underdeveloped countries in our global economy. The produce is likely to be handled by a hepatitis A virus carrier and washed with contaminated water before being shipped. Consumers in developed countries risk ingestion of contaminated food. For example, 600 people were infected by hepatitis A after eating contaminated onions at a single restaurant in Pennsylvania. The onions were imported from Mexico, where the incidence of hepatitis A is high.

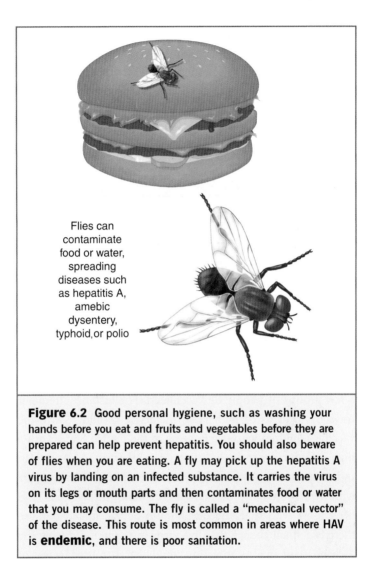

Flies can contaminate food or water, spreading diseases such as hepatitis A, amebic dysentery, typhoid,or polio

Figure 6.2 Good personal hygiene, such as washing your hands before you eat and fruits and vegetables before they are prepared can help prevent hepatitis. You should also beware of flies when you are eating. A fly may pick up the hepatitis A virus by landing on an infected substance. It carries the virus on its legs or mouth parts and then contaminates food or water that you may consume. The fly is called a "mechanical vector" of the disease. This route is most common in areas where HAV is **endemic**, and there is poor sanitation.

reduce the incidence of the disease dramatically. Public water in the United States is safe. Caution about foods is also appropriate. Avoid eating fresh fruits and vegetables and raw shellfish in underdeveloped countries unless you have been immunized. Anal intercourse should be avoided unless a condom is used or both partners have been immunized.

It is possible to receive temporary immunization from an injection of the immunoglobulin IgG-A. This protection lasts only as long as the IgG remains in the blood, which is about 2 to 3 months, because the B cells are not stimulated to produce the antibody. Stimulation of B cells can only be done by an HAV antigen. This approach works well to stop an acute infection when it is known that HAV exposure has occurred within the past 2 weeks. It is a useful preventive approach for a person planning to travel to areas with high disease incidence and remain for a short time. People who must depart on a trip quickly may not have time to develop immunity from a vaccination and may take advantage of IgG-A.

Permanent immunization with a vaccine lasts a lifetime. Vaccination is not recommended for all people in developed countries like the United States because the incidence of HAV is low and the cost per person for the vaccine is fairly high. The cost in this country is about $50 per dose. This cost is prohibitive in poor countries. In the United States, the Centers for Disease Control and Prevention (CDC) recommends that only a few groups of people be vaccinated. For instance, frequent travelers to areas of high HAV incidence should receive the vaccine. Children who live in areas of the United States with a high HAV incidence, including poor rural areas and American Indian reservations, should be vaccinated. Men who have sex with men should also be vaccinated. Finally, intravenous (IV) drug users who share needles should be vaccinated because there is a small chance that live virus in the blood during the early phase of an HAV infection could be transmitted by way of a syringe needle.

7

Hepatitis B

VALERIE AND DAVID

Valerie, a young newlywed and 6 months pregnant, worked as a nurse at a large hospital. She scratched her finger early one morning while pruning a rose bush in her garden. She thought nothing of it and didn't bother to bandage the scratch. That afternoon, she went to work. A patient who had his blood drawn accidentally dropped on the floor the gauze pad that he used to press over the needle puncture site. Valerie quickly picked up the pad and put it in the medical waste bin. She wasn't wearing gloves at the time but thought she had been careful, and she washed her hands immediately afterward.

Three months later, Valerie gave birth to a beautiful baby boy, David. David had a healthy, normal childhood and grew up to be a strapping young man. One day David decided to donate blood in response to an urgent plea for donors from the local hospital. This was his first experience donating blood and he was nervous, but all went well and he left the hospital feeling good about helping others. About a week later, he received a letter from the hospital that said a test of his blood revealed that he could be a carrier for the hepatitis B virus (HBV). He was urged to consult his doctor.

David did not have any of the standard symptoms of acute hepatitis. His doctor ordered liver function tests for ALT, bilirubin, and other chemicals (see Chapter 1), which were normal; a coagulation test for blood clotting; and a blood test for the hepatitis B surface antigen (HBsAg), which was positive. The doctor agreed that David was probably a carrier of HBV. Since David had no symptoms and there is no treatment for the disease, the doctor advised him about precautions he should take to avoid transmission of the virus to others. He also interviewed David at length to determine how he may have been infected. Neither one of them could come up with a plausible scenario. David was scheduled to return to the doctor in 6 months for follow-up blood and liver function tests in order to determine whether he was a carrier with a chronic infection.

David was not one to sit around and wait for things to happen. He set about to learn all he could about his disease and tried to figure out how he fit into the picture. He also tried to find clues about how he could have been infected. He had to tell his family about his illness anyway, so he decided to ask them for ideas about the infection route. Valerie was upset by the news. As a nurse, she understood how HBV is transmitted. Neither she nor David's father and sisters had ever had symptoms or been diagnosed with hepatitis. She decided to have all of them tested for HBV. Of the five, only Valerie tested positive for the HBV immunoglobulins IgG anti-HBs and IgG anti-HBc, which are produced in response to HBsAg and the core antigen HBcAg, respectively. Both antibodies usually persist for a lifetime if the person recovers. Valerie realized that she must have had an acute, symptom-free HBV infection, possibly when she was pregnant, and may have given the virus to David. She could not recall how she was infected, but knew that as a nurse, she could have been exposed to the virus many times. She also knew that chronic hepatitis B can ultimately cause cirrhosis or liver cancer. She was extremely upset and felt very guilty. David consoled his mother and reassured her that he did not blame her. It had just happened. He, too, was upset, of course, and continued to learn more about the disease.

Most children and at least half of all adults who are infected with HBV never experience the classic hepatitis symptoms. Neither Valerie nor David ever had symptoms. It is a mystery why symptoms do not occur, although it is known that the virus itself does not kill the host hepatocytes. Only the killer T cells do that, and they are the principal weapons of the immune response. It is possible that in many cases, the immune system gets the virus under control before enough damage is done to cause symptoms. About 90% of infected children and adults recover, as Valerie did. David was one of the unlucky 10%. However, about 80% of newborns develop chronic hepatitis, possibly because a newborn's immune system is not fully developed.

ABOUT HBV

The blood work from David's 6-month follow-up visit was still positive for HBsAg. This result is considered diagnostic of a chronic HBV infection (see Chapter 2). The chronic phase develops when the immune system is unable to detect the virus in the hepatocytes. The virus can change its epitopes, for example, so that the B cells and killer T cells no longer recognize them as antigens (see Chapter 4). David is a carrier and will be contagious for many years. This fact severely limits his lifestyle because transmission of the virus involves exposure to infected blood or other body fluids. There are many precautions he has to take: He cannot donate blood. He should not participate in sports or other activities in which others could come into contact with his blood, sweat, tears, or saliva. Sports such as basketball, football, soccer, wrestling, and hockey should be avoided, although tennis, golf, and skiing are safe. He will have to clean his dishes and eating utensils very carefully to protect his family and friends. He will have to take great care to prevent exposing family members to his blood. For example, if he has open wounds or sores, or cuts himself while shaving and a drop of blood is left in the sink, a family member may come into contact with the virus. He should always use a condom when having sex and, thus, may not have children. He will have to see his doctor regularly so that both of them can follow the progress of the disease and watch for complications.

In the chronic phase of HBV, the virus continues to impair liver function and cause inflammation at modest levels. David could be symptom-free for 10 or more years. It is the cumulative effects of the killer T cells killing the hepatocytes over many years that ultimately cause serious liver damage. Time is the enemy in the chronic phase. Cirrhosis develops in about 30% of hepatitis B cases, and liver cancer develops in about 20% of cases after 10 years.

HBV

The hepatitis B virus is classified as an hepadnavirus. It is the only hepatitis virus that has DNA as its nucleic acid. Its nucleocapsid is spherical, as are those of all known hepatitis viruses, and it has an envelope. The envelope itself can have many shapes. Figure 7.1 is an illustration of the virion. The surface antigen HBsAg is in the envelope and its presence in blood is diagnostic of an active infection. Another antigen, HBcAg, is called a **core antigen** (part of the "core," or essential structure, of the virus) and can be very difficult to detect directly because it is shielded from the outside world by the envelope and the capsid. However, antibodies to HBcAg can be found in people with chronic infections or in those who have recovered from an acute infection. HBsAg can first show up in blood during the incubation phase a few weeks after the infection or may not appear until the completion of the prodromal phase a month or so later, but it is always the first antigen to appear in the blood. It persists in the blood during a chronic infection. (The tests used for antigens and antibodies are described in Chapter 4.)

ROUTES OF HBV TRANSMISSION

HBV is a bloodborne virus that can leave the blood and enter other body fluids such as saliva, semen, tears, sweat, and vaginal fluids. HBV cannot survive in the intestines very well because the virus is attacked and destroyed by the bacteria that normally live there. Valerie had an acute infection from which she recovered, but we know that the infection could have been active during David's birth because of her handling of the bloody gauze and the scratch on her finger. David probably

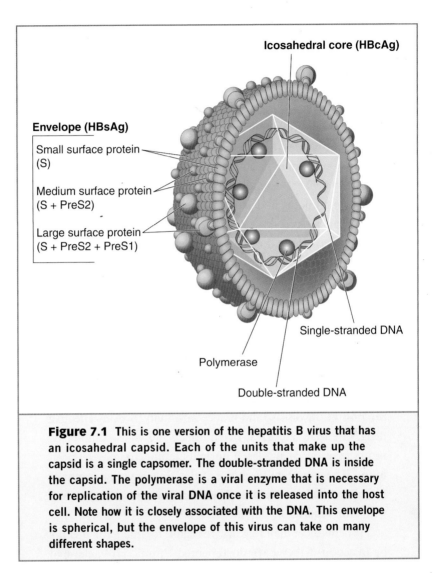

Icosahedral core (HBcAg)

Envelope (HBsAg)

Small surface protein (S)

Medium surface protein (S + PreS2)

Large surface protein (S + PreS2 + PreS1)

Single-stranded DNA

Polymerase

Double-stranded DNA

Figure 7.1 This is one version of the hepatitis B virus that has an icosahedral capsid. Each of the units that make up the capsid is a single capsomer. The double-stranded DNA is inside the capsid. The polymerase is a viral enzyme that is necessary for replication of the viral DNA once it is released into the host cell. Note how it is closely associated with the DNA. This envelope is spherical, but the envelope of this virus can take on many different shapes.

acquired his infection from Valerie's vaginal fluids at birth. This infection route is very common wherever the disease is endemic (common in a specific area). It is unlikely that David got the virus directly from his mother's blood because the virus does not cross the placenta and there is no other way he could have been exposed to Valerie's blood while in her womb.

HBV is considered more infectious than HIV, the virus that causes AIDS. Transmission from mother to child at birth is a common route. Needle-sharing among drug abusers is another common route, especially in developed countries. Sex with an infected person is dangerous. Accidental touching of infected body fluids and then touching the mouth, eyes, or broken skin is another route. Accidental needle punctures or scalpel cuts are serious occupational hazards for health-care workers. Another route is by deliberate puncture with improperly cleaned needles, such as in tattooing and acupuncture. Tools used in nail salons and barbershops can be contaminated, and this risk is especially high in areas where the virus is endemic. Finally, the sharing of toiletry articles such as toothbrushes, razors, razor blades, fingernail files, or nail clippers with family members can expose a person to the virus if the person has a cut or open sore that touches the contaminated tool or toiletry article.

TREATMENT

The acute phase of HBV is not treatable other than for symptom relief. Treatment for the chronic disease seeks to slow the progress of the disease and reduce infectivity. A really effective drug, one that can arrest or eliminate the virus completely, promote recovery, and last a normal lifetime, has not yet been found. The treatment of choice at this time is with a group of proteins called **interferons**. These are proteins that interfere with viral replication (Figure 7.2).

Patients older than 18 years are eligible for interferon therapy by injection if they have documented chronic HBV, elevated liver enzymes such as ALT, and an active virus in the blood. Interferon-α treatment lasts for about 16 weeks. A long-term remission of the disease is achieved in about 35% of cases, with a return to normal liver enzyme levels and reduced infectivity.

A new drug, called lamivudine, that interferes with virus replication has shown some promise but its effectiveness after one year has not yet been established. It is still experimental

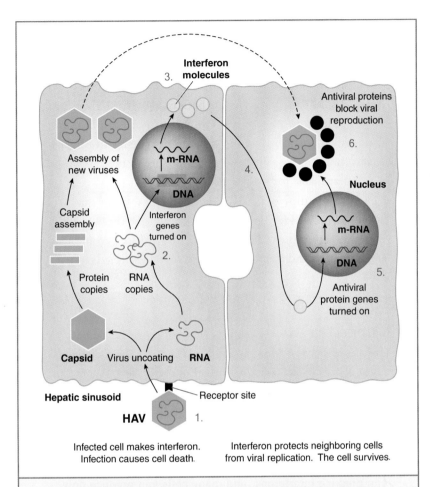

Figure 7.2 This diagram shows how interferon works. A virus binds to a host cell and inserts its nucleic acid into the cytoplasm (1). The normal viral replication process is started. However, the cell reacts to the invader by turning on the interferon gene in its own DNA (2). Interferon is thus synthesized by the cell (3). Interferon can leave the infected cell and enter neighboring cells (4), where it activates production of antiviral proteins by that cell (5). These proteins can then intercept invading viruses and block further viral reproduction (6). Synthetic interferons may be injected as a method of fighting the hepatitis B virus because host hepatocytes do not produce them. Thus, only steps (4) and (5) occur in this case.

but is not known to cause serious side effects. The treatment with lamivudine consists of taking one tablet by mouth daily. This is a lot easier than receiving a regular series of painful injections of interferon for four months. However, the patient must take the drug for a lifetime because the drug only arrests viral replication; it does not kill the virus. A combination therapy with interferon-α and lamivudine is being investigated at this time and has shown some promising results. However, it is not available for routine use.

Adefovir dipivoxil (Hepsera®) is a new drug that was approved in 2002 for treatment of chronic HBV in the United States. It can improve liver function and reduce chronic liver inflammation and scarring by 50% to 65% in selected patients.

INTERFERONS

Interferons are immune proteins that are produced by host cells in response to viral infections. There are three distinct types of interferons called α (alpha), β (beta), and γ (gamma). They stimulate host cells to produce proteins that inhibit the replication of viral nucleic acid and the synthesis of viral proteins. Thus, they "interfere" with viral reproduction without killing the virus directly. Interferons also activate helper T cells and accelerate the activity of the B cells. Not all cells can produce interferons, and many cells can produce only one kind. White blood cells, for example, produce both α and β proteins. The interferon system does not always work well, and much research is devoted to understanding how it is regulated and how it may be activated by drugs. Other efforts are being made to use interferons as injectable drugs for a number of viral diseases, including hepatitis. Interferons α-2a and α-2b are approved in the United States for use in hepatitis B patients. These drugs do not always work, but they can be more effective than other drugs and may be the best that can be done at the present time.

The drug interferes with viral replication like lamivudine, but it seems to work better. It has not been studied for use with interferon, and it can have serious side effects, including kidney damage. In addition, in 25% of patients, discontinuation of use can cause a viral rebound that makes the disease even worse than before treatment.

David was eligible for interferon therapy and decided to try it despite the low success rate of the treatment and its side effects. Interferon can cause fever, fatigue, malaise, and suppression of white blood cells, but these effects disappear when the treatment is complete. He did suffer from fatigue and fever during the treatment, and he lost quite a bit of time from work because of it. However, upon completion of the treatment, he had no detectable viral DNA or viral antigens in his blood. The outlook for permanent remission was good and David was elated. He would have to be monitored at least yearly for the rest of his life to be on guard for a recurrence of virus activity.

WORLDWIDE OCCURRENCE AND PREVENTION.

The World Health Organization estimates that about 2 billion people alive today have been infected with HBV. Nearly 350 million of these people are carriers. Hepatitis B is the most serious and important viral hepatitis in the world because there are so many carriers, it is so contagious, and its severe effects in the chronic phase cause terrible suffering and impose huge costs for medical care. Underdeveloped countries have the highest incidence because of lack of funds for vaccines and poor public health services. However, in the United States and other developed countries, less than 20% of the population has been infected and less than 2% are carriers (perhaps 1 million people). The lower incidence is due to a very effective vaccination program and screening of donated blood. Post-transfusion hepatitis B is rare in the United States. Neither Valerie nor David had been vaccinated, because until about 10 years ago, it was thought that the low incidence of the disease did not justify the cost of routine vaccination. Vaccination would not have helped David anyway, since he picked up the virus at birth.

An effective vaccine for hepatitis B has been available for only about 20 years. The World Health Organization now recommends that all newborns be vaccinated for both hepatitis A and B, but this has not been feasible in many parts of the world because of the high cost and the difficulty of reaching people in remote areas. It has been standard practice in the United States and Europe to screen all pregnant women and vaccinate all newborns for hepatitis B only since 1991.

An unvaccinated adult should be vaccinated if he or she is at risk for exposure to HBV. Adults who may have frequent,

INCIDENCE, PREVALENCE, ENDEMIC, AND OUTBREAK

When health professionals talk about the occurrence of a disease in some part of the world, they try to use language that can be understood by all health professionals and to present information that allows comparison with occurrences elsewhere. *Incidence* refers to the number of new cases per year for a specified number of people, which could be 100, or 1,000, or 1 million people. It is not essential to know what the actual population size is when we express things this way. For example, the incidence of hepatitis B in the United States in 2002 was about 2.8 cases per 100,000 people per year, but that number may have been derived from a survey of the entire U.S. population. **Prevalence** is similar to incidence, except that the statistic includes all cases, new and old, per year. *Endemic* means that a disease has a fairly constant incidence over a long period of time. The level of incidence does not influence the decision to call a disease endemic in a geographical location as long as that incidence is above the average for areas with low direct contact with carriers, such as health-care workers, drug users, police officers, and firefighters, as well as those who travel frequently to areas where HBV is endemic, should be vaccinated. An immunoglobulin specific for HBV is available but very expensive. It provides only short-term protection against infection and is recommended for newborns of mothers who are carriers, in addition to vaccination, and for adults who know they have been exposed to the virus within the past three days because it can work effectively to destroy the virus within that very narrow time frame. The World Health Organization has set a long-term goal of universal vaccination. It is working on financial, cultural, and political strategies to realize this goal.

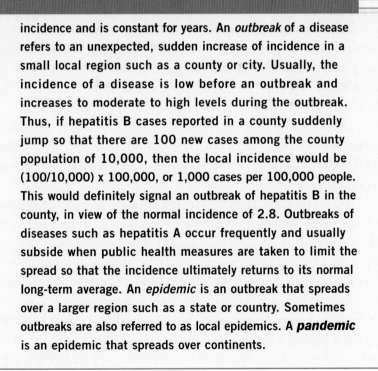

incidence and is constant for years. An *outbreak* of a disease refers to an unexpected, sudden increase of incidence in a small local region such as a county or city. Usually, the incidence of a disease is low before an outbreak and increases to moderate to high levels during the outbreak. Thus, if hepatitis B cases reported in a county suddenly jump so that there are 100 new cases among the county population of 10,000, then the local incidence would be (100/10,000) x 100,000, or 1,000 cases per 100,000 people. This would definitely signal an outbreak of hepatitis B in the county, in view of the normal incidence of 2.8. Outbreaks of diseases such as hepatitis A occur frequently and usually subside when public health measures are taken to limit the spread so that the incidence ultimately returns to its normal long-term average. An *epidemic* is an outbreak that spreads over a larger region such as a state or country. Sometimes outbreaks are also referred to as local epidemics. A **pandemic** is an epidemic that spreads over continents.

8

Hepatitis D

Hepatitis D is discussed here before hepatitis C because it is very closely associated with hepatitis B, as you will see.

A NEW HEPATITIS ANTIGEN

A new antigen was discovered in 1977 in the hepatocytes of a hepatitis B patient in Italy. The protein resembled the hepatitis B core antigen HBcAg (Chapter 7) in that it could be found only inside the host hepatocytes of patients with hepatitis B. However, the antigen was distinct from any known HBV antigen and was given the special name "delta antigen" because it was thought to be another HBV antigen. It was soon learned that patients with delta antigen produced antibodies to it. In 1980, the delta antigen was established as part of a new microbe, which was called the hepatitis delta virus. It is now more commonly called the hepatitis D virus (HDV), and the disease it causes is called hepatitis D. The unique feature of this virus is that it can cause hepatitis only with the assistance of HBV. HDV can cause very severe forms of acute and chronic hepatitis in patients with chronic hepatitis B.

HDV is rare in the United States and northern Europe, but common in countries surrounding the Mediterranean Sea and in Eastern Europe, Russia, some central African countries, and some Latin American countries (Figure 8.1). The lower incidence may be because the incidence of hepatitis B is much lower in the United States and Europe than elsewhere, thanks to effective vaccination and blood screening programs. Epidemics have occurred among some native Venezuelan tribes, in areas surrounding the Amazon River, in Mediterranean countries, and in central Africa. HDV is endemic in Mediterranean countries. A high prevalence of

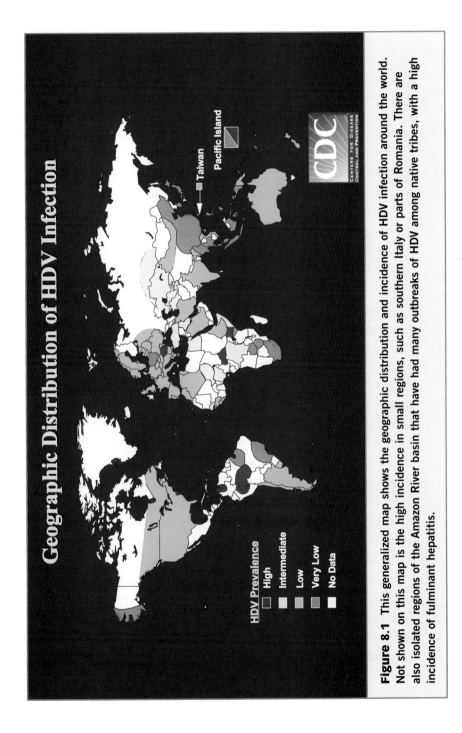

Figure 8.1 This generalized map shows the geographic distribution and incidence of HDV infection around the world. Not shown on this map is the high incidence in small regions, such as southern Italy or parts of Romania. There are also isolated regions of the Amazon River basin that have had many outbreaks of HDV among native tribes, with a high incidence of fulminant hepatitis.

HDV has been found recently in Albania, in some parts of China, in northern India, and in Okinawa. The World Health Organization estimates that more than 10 million people are infected with HDV worldwide. However, in countries that have adopted a stringent HBV control program, the prevalence of HDV is similar to that of HBV.

ABOUT HDV

HDV is unusual because it has single-stranded RNA that forms a closed circle and is the only known mammalian virus that does so. Its nucleocapsid has no well-defined structure, although it is probably spherical. The capsid has 60 copies of one protein, the delta antigen, HDAg. HDAg is the only protein encoded by the nucleic acid and is necessary for replication of the viral RNA and assembly of new virions. The nucleocapsid is enclosed by an envelope, but there are no spikes of HDAg on the surface. Thus, the immune system cannot easily recognize HDV as a new microbe. The envelope of HDV contains only the three forms of the HBV antigen HBsAg. This protein is essential for binding HDV to host cell receptors, for penetrating the host cell, and for assembling virions in the host. Some scientists consider HDV a subviral satellite of HBV (see box on page 79).

HDV cannot reproduce without the help of HBV. It has no enzymes in the nucleocapsid and does not have genes for the enzymes that are needed for replication and protein synthesis in the host cell. HBV provides the necessary enzymes for replication and thus is a "helper virus" for HDV. When HDV is replicating in the host cell, HBV replication is turned off by HDAg. HDV commandeers all the HBV replication proteins.

TRANSMISSION OF HDV

To be infected by HDV, a person must also have HBV. HDV infection can occur in one of two ways. First, both viruses may infect at the same time. This is known as a **coinfection**. Second, a person with a chronic HBV infection can be exposed to HDV and become infected. This is known as a **superinfection**. HDV is a bloodborne virus like HBV and is transmitted in much the same way. The most common route of infection is by infected blood and blood products. Sharing of needles by intravenous drug abusers is another common route, especially in the United States and Europe. Unprotected sex, especially without a condom, is another route of transmission, especially worldwide. However, transmission from mother to newborn does not seem to occur.

COURSE OF THE DISEASE

The course of HDV depends on the way it is acquired. With coinfection (Figure 8.2), both acute hepatitis B and D develop.

VIROIDS AND SATELLITE VIRUSES

Viroids are infectious, virus-like microbes that have a single-stranded RNA that forms a closed circle; they have no capsid. The nucleic acid does not code for any proteins and must be replicated by the host cell. A helper virus for replication is not needed. Viroids infect plant cells and are a common problem in horticulture and agriculture. No viroids have been found in mammals, although some viruses that infect humans are similar to viroids. For example, hepatitis D virus is the only virus found in humans that has single-stranded circular RNA.

Satellite viruses, also called virusoids, have single-stranded RNA that forms a closed circle like that in viroids. Unlike viroids, the RNA encodes its own capsid protein. Satellite viruses replicate in the host cell cytoplasm using an RNA enzyme that is commonly found in plant cell cytoplasm but not in mammalian cell cytoplasm, and they require a helper virus to form their capsids. The RNA does code for some proteins. Similar viruses that infect animals, including humans, are also called satellite viruses because they must be closely associated with a helper virus. The hepatitis D virus is an excellent example of a satellite virus that infects humans.

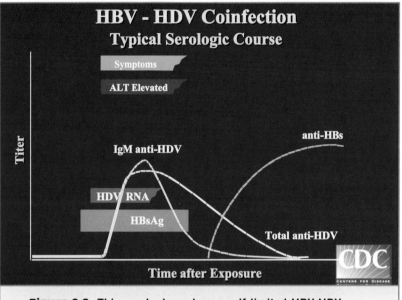

Figure 8.2 This graph shows how a self-limited HBV-HDV coinfection develops over time. "Titer" refers to the blood serum level of each substance. The horizontal bars indicate the time period over which the specified items can be observed or measured. Note that HbsAg and HDV RNA appear in the serum at about the same time during the incubation period. This is the most communicable stage of the disease, since the person is unaware he or she has the infection despite the very active virus in the blood. HBsAg (orange bar) disappears after a while, indicating that the person's immune system has successfully fought off the infection. The serum titer of anti-HBs (orange line) rises and remains high, which indicates a developed immunity for HBV. Since HDV and HBV are tied together, HDV-related substances rise initially and then disappear. That is what happens for the IgM anti-HDV (yellow line) and total anti-HDV (blue line) titers. Serum HDV RNA also disappears (magenta bar) when HBV declines, because HDV can not reproduce.

If the dose of HBV is large, symptoms develop and run their course at about the same time. If the HBV dose is small, hepatitis B develops first and starts to resolve before hepatitis D expresses symptoms. In the latter case, the acute phase of the diseases lasts somewhat longer than if only an HBV infection had occurred. Coinfections are usually self-limited because the immune response to HBV effectively stops both viruses. Progression to chronic hepatitis D occurs in only 5% of cases.

Symptoms due to coinfection are likely to be more severe than for HBV alone. Disabling fatigue, lethargy, anorexia, and nausea develop first and last for 3 to 7 days. Jaundice may then set in. Fatigue and nausea continue, urine turns dark yellow, and the stool becomes clay-colored. Symptoms subside as the immune system eliminates HBV, but fatigue may last longer than the other symptoms and prolong recovery time.

Superinfection is a far more serious process (Figure 8.3). Severe acute hepatitis D infection leads to chronic hepatitis D in 80% of cases. This happens because the immune system of a person with chronic hepatitis B has not been successful in eliminating the virus. In this case, HBV is always available to help HDV reproduce. During the early stage of superinfection, HBV replication is suppressed by HDV, and the D virus replicates. It is not understood why, but later, HDV replication subsides and HBV replication resumes. Symptoms during the chronic phase of hepatitis D are less severe than during the acute phase. Finally, late in the disease, either both viruses become inactive and remission occurs, or one or both of the viruses remain active. If both viruses remain active, then within 10 years, cirrhosis and liver cancer can develop as a result of chronic inflammation of the liver. These complications develop much more rapidly than with HBV alone. About 60% to 70% of patients with chronic hepatitis D develop cirrhosis and most die from liver failure. Fulminant hepatitis, though rare, is 10 times more likely to develop with a superinfection by HDV than with any other hepatitis virus infection. About 80% of patients with fulminant hepatitis die unless they can receive a liver transplant. About 20% of all patients with HDV die—a mortality rate about 10 times higher than that for HBV infection alone.

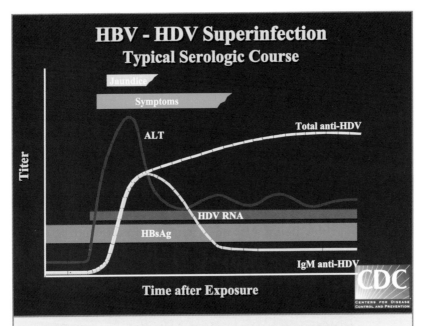

Figure 8.3 This diagram shows the course of HBV-HDV super-infection over time. "Titer" refers to the blood serum level of each substance. The time refers to the time after exposure to HDV. The person has already acquired a chronic HBV infection. Note that there is an incubation period for HDV. This is a typical record of a patient who has chronic hepatitis. The HBsAg titer (orange bar) is measurable but lower than for a pure HBV infection because HDV interferes with HBV reproduction. HDV RNA (magenta bar) appears and remains measurable because the infection is chronic. The IgM anti-HDV (yellow line) appears first, which is normal, but remains at measurable levels because the infection is chronic. Total anti-HDV (blue line) antibodies rise slowly and remain elevated due to the persistence of HDV. Note the high levels of serum ALT (red line) that indicate ongoing liver damage. Superinfections are far more serious than coinfections because they always result in chronic hepatitis with more severe symptoms that persist longer (green bar) and a very high risk of liver failure or liver cancer.

TREATMENT

No antiviral therapies are available for treatment of either acute or chronic hepatitis D. Interferon-α therapy (Chapter 7), which targets the HBV, slows the progress of the disease and has caused remissions. But the therapy does not make the patient virus-free. An interferon-treated patient remains a carrier of HDV.

PREVENTION

The best way to prevent an HDV infection is to be vaccinated for HBV. People should take all the precautions recommended to avoid exposure to HBV (see Chapter 7). Anyone with chronic hepatitis B must be educated about the risks of acquiring HDV. Sharing of drug injection needles and unprotected sex are the two most important behaviors that should be avoided; the consequences of reckless behavior are severe.

9

Hepatitis C

KEVIN

Kevin was a 30-year-old African-American attorney working for a large law firm in Chicago. He became interested in his roots and started exploring his family history. He started with a family Bible that had been passed down from the time of the Civil War (1861–1865). He found that his great-great-great-grandfather was a slave on a plantation in Mississippi. So Kevin went to Jackson, Mississippi, and searched the public records stored down in a musty basement. He found that most slaves in that region came from West Africa in what is now the modern country of the Gambia. He could not find any information about his ancestor, but decided to visit the Gambia on his next vacation to pursue his roots further. Kevin learned to his delight that the Gambia is a terrific vacation destination. Situated on the Atlantic coast, it has a balmy climate year-round, miles of beautiful beaches, excellent hotels, very friendly English-speaking people, and few crowds of tourists.

Kevin was excited about his trip. He flew to Banjul, the capital city of the Gambia. But on the way to his hotel, the taxi he was riding in was involved in a terrible accident. Kevin was severely injured and was rushed to the hospital in Banjul. He needed emergency surgery and required a transfusion of 1 unit of blood. The surgery went well. Kevin's surgeon had trained at the University of Chicago Medical School, which took Kevin by surprise, so the two of them had lots to talk about.

Kevin spent the rest of his vacation in Banjul recuperating from the accident and the surgery. After flying home, he felt much better and was ready to return to work three weeks later. But all was not well. Three months after his return to work, Kevin began to feel unusually tired. He was an athletic person, but he could no longer finish a game of racquetball. He found it increasingly difficult to get through a typically busy day at the office. Kevin just thought he was in a slump after his trip and accident and that he would get over it soon enough. Then his wife noticed that the whites of his eyes were yellowed. She insisted that he go to see his doctor.

Kevin had only two of the symptoms of acute hepatitis—jaundice and fatigue—but his doctor suspected the disease when he heard about Kevin's trip to an underdeveloped country. Kevin could have been exposed to a hepatitis virus during the accident, during surgery, or from the blood transfusion. He also could have been exposed to one of the enteric viruses (viruses introduced through the intestine). Kevin had chosen to be immunized for hepatitides A and B before he went on his trip. A blood test was ordered for hepatitis C, and for hepatitides A and B, just in case the original vaccinations had not been effective. Results showed that Kevin had anti-HAV IgG, an antibody for HAV that is expected after recovery from an acute phase illness or after immunization. Of the three antibodies for HBV, the tests found anti-HBs and anti-HBc, but not anti-HBsAG. This pattern is expected after immunization. In addition, a second-generation enzyme immunoassay (EIA-2) was positive for hepatitis C antibodies. A follow-up recombinant immunoblot assay (RIBA-2) for HCV antigens was also positive and confirmed the EIA-2 results. These two

UNIT OF BLOOD

A unit of blood is a standard volume of blood that is recognized everywhere. A standard volume is necessary so that health workers all over the world know exactly how much blood they have available. One bag of blood, collected at a blood donor center or at a hospital, contains roughly 1 pint and comprises a standard unit of blood.

tests (see Chapter 4) became routinely available in the United States and other developed countries only in 1992.

The finding was that Kevin had acute hepatitis C. He was devastated and couldn't accept the diagnosis. He knew how serious the disease is and thought only intravenous drug abusers could get it. He sought a second opinion, just to be sure, and the diagnosis was confirmed. He realized he had to learn more about his illness. As he learned and understood more about how he became infected and how the disease can be managed, he gained hope that his future was not as grim as he thought at first.

ABOUT THE VIRUS

The hepatitis C virus (HCV) is classified as a flavivirus. It is a bloodborne, spherical virus with an icosahedral capsid and an envelope. The nucleocapsid contains a single-stranded RNA. The detailed structure of HCV is not known, probably because it was identified as a unique virus only in 1988 and is very difficult to isolate for structural studies. The viral RNA encodes a single, huge protein that is called a **polyprotein** because it is made up of several different proteins that are linked together end-to-end. After synthesis, the polyprotein is broken down by cell enzymes into 10 smaller structural and regulatory proteins. Core proteins and two envelope proteins are especially important products of this breakdown, as are several enzymes that are important for viral replication.

RNA-polymerase is a very important enzyme for replication of viral RNA, but the HCV enzyme has a defect. It is not able to detect errors during synthesis of new RNA like most other enymes of this kind. It may not notice, for example, if the code for the amino acid glycine is substituted by the code for the amino acid alanine in the replicating RNA. This defect actually works to the advantage of the HCV. There are two regions on the envelope protein E2 that have an extremely high mutation rate, thanks to this enzyme defect. Therefore, many mutants can be generated quickly, allowing HCV to evade attack by the immune system. Development of a vaccine for HCV has not been successful because vaccines are designed to mimic specific epitopes and thereby elicit an immune response with production of antibodies. It takes so long to develop and test a vaccine that by the time it is ready for use the virus has mutated and is unrecognizable to the antibodies induced by the vaccine. It is also thought that another enzyme encoded by the viral RNA specifically inhibits a critically important immune system molecule known as interferon-3 (INF-3). The loss of INF-3 activity effectively shuts down the immune response to HCV and allows the virus to replicate freely.

There are six major HCV **genotypes** (genetic makeup of an individual) with subtypes. Types 1, 2, and 3 are distributed worldwide, whereas the others have more localized distributions. Type 1b is most common in the United States and is associated with the more severe forms of the disease. Doctors seek to determine the virus genotype when they know a patient is infected with HCV because the duration and success of treatment depend on the type. Most Americans who are infected in the United States have type 1b, but Kevin had type 2 because he acquired it in Africa, where it is common. Type 1 infections require 12 months of treatment; all other types require only 6 months. Knowledge of the length of time needed for treatment is important because the entire treatment process is expensive and unpleasant.

HCV reproduction is very fast. A trillion (1 million-million) new virions can be made in a day, so that virus-free hepatocytes can be infected very quickly after the initial infection. Within days, at least half of all hepatocytes (liver cells) can be infected.

During the acute phase of HCV infection, the symptoms are mild. Only 10% of those infected have any symptoms at all. Kevin had two symptoms, and the fatigue was disabling. However, he was lucky, because his symptoms enabled early detection of the disease. He might have been a symptom-free carrier who discovered his illness years after liver damage was very advanced and he was showing signs of liver failure.

The immune system is not very successful in defeating the HCV virus. At least 80% of those infected develop the chronic disease. The primary immune response is cellular, involving killer T cells. The liver becomes chronically inflamed. Over a span of 10 to 20 years, scarring of the liver can develop into cirrhosis in 10% to 20% of infected people. Liver cancer develops in about 5% of victims after 30 years.

TRANSMISSION

HCV was originally called a non-A, non-B virus because it could not be isolated, yet it was known that a microbe caused a unique form of hepatitis. The virus was finally identified in 1989, and a reliable diagnostic test was developed in 1990. Routine screening of all donated blood became possible in developed countries in 1992. Before 1992, the most common route of transmission was by blood transfusion. Back then, the cause of hepatitis after blood transfusion was unknown, but it always developed after a blood transfusion and was called post-transfusion hepatitis (Figure 9.1). Routine screening of donated blood in advanced countries has eliminated this route of transmission. But because of the high cost and limited lab facilities for routine screening, blood transfusion is the main mode of transmission in under-developed countries. The Gambia does not routinely screen blood for HCV even though its incidence is high in that part of Africa. Kevin unfortunately received a unit of blood that contained the virus and had not been screened.

HCV is transmitted almost exclusively by direct intro-duction of infected blood into the body (Figure 9.2), unlike transmission of HBV. In fact, HBV is far more infectious than HCV. Use of dirty needles by intravenous drug abusers is a very common cause of infection in the United States and other developed countries. Acupuncture and tattooing with improperly cleaned instruments and sharing a razor with an

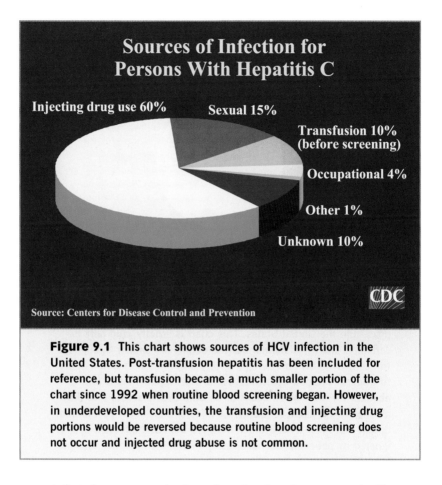

Sources of Infection for Persons With Hepatitis C

Injecting drug use 60%

Sexual 15%

Transfusion 10% (before screening)

Occupational 4%

Other 1%

Unknown 10%

Source: Centers for Disease Control and Prevention

CDC

Figure 9.1 This chart shows sources of HCV infection in the United States. Post-transfusion hepatitis has been included for reference, but transfusion became a much smaller portion of the chart since 1992 when routine blood screening began. However, in underdeveloped countries, the transfusion and injecting drug portions would be reversed because routine blood screening does not occur and injected drug abuse is not common.

infected person can also introduce the virus, but are not significant routes of infection. You might expect that accidental needle punctures or scalpel cuts in health-care workers would be an important route of infection, but there is no evidence that these people have an above-average incidence of HCV. They tend to be very careful.

TREATMENT

There is no treatment for acute HCV other than symptom relief. Late-stage liver failure is often treated with a liver transplant, but this does not eliminate the disease. A transplant just buys

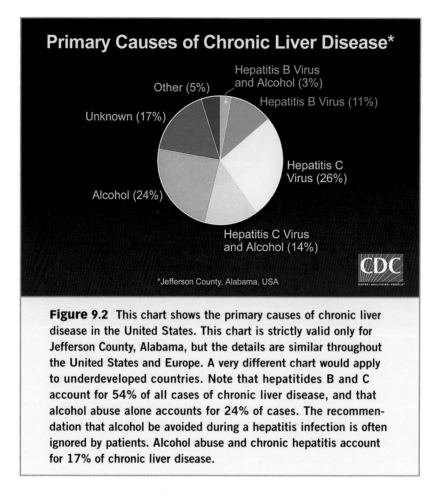

Figure 9.2 This chart shows the primary causes of chronic liver disease in the United States. This chart is strictly valid only for Jefferson County, Alabama, but the details are similar throughout the United States and Europe. A very different chart would apply to underdeveloped countries. Note that hepatitides B and C account for 54% of all cases of chronic liver disease, and that alcohol abuse alone accounts for 24% of cases. The recommendation that alcohol be avoided during a hepatitis infection is often ignored by patients. Alcohol abuse and chronic hepatitis account for 17% of chronic liver disease.

the patient more quality time, although that can be very significant and worth the trouble.

Specific antiviral drugs have been developed that show promise for treating the chronic disease, but they are extremely expensive. A combination of **pegylated** (man-made) interferon-α-2a or -2b (see box on page 91) and ribavirin can be an effective antiviral treatment.

Treatment of chronic disease can eliminate the virus from the blood in up to 50% of those infected with the type 1 virus and in up to 80% of those infected with virus types 2 or 3.

PEG, INTERFERON, AND RIBAVIRIN REGIMEN

Interferon therapy for hepatitis C has been disappointing. Although positive effects are obtained, these effects do not last. The procedure requires daily, or at best three times weekly, injections of the drug for up to one year. Side effects in some patients often require cessation of therapy. A new approach is now used. A molecule called polyethylene glycol (PEG) can be attached to an interferon α-2b protein to create PEG-IFN. This artificial pegylated interferon is more stable chemically in the blood, so only one injection per week is needed. Patients treated with this new drug have a much higher chance for a successful arrest of the virus than patients treated with IFN-α-2b alone.

Ribavirin is a drug that can be taken orally. It mimics the bases that are key parts of nucleic acid structure and interferes with proper reproduction of the viral RNA. It does not work for hepatitis C patients when given by itself, but when it is given in combination with PEG-IFN, it improves the success rate of the therapy. It also causes side effects in some patients, which may require cessation of therapy.

Combination therapy with PEG-IFN-α-2b and ribavirin is now the treatment of choice for chronic hepatitis C patients. It may also be used for patients in the acute disease phase, although this strategy is still being tested. In clinical trials, up to 20% of patients receiving combination therapy were unable to tolerate it. The treatment does not produce a cure, but removes the virus from the blood and retards or arrests the progression of the disease. An average success rate of 60% of those treated has been achieved, and scientists are working on ways to improve this rate.

Elimination from the blood does not mean that the virus has been eliminated from all hepatocytes. It only means that virus replication has been slowed down and is less likely to cause serious liver malfunction or failure. Treated HCV carriers are also less infectious, although they definitely should not donate blood or organs. Such patients must be checked regularly for recurrence of an active infection. It may be necessary to repeat the treatment in the event of a recurrence. Serious side effects can be caused by the antiviral treatment, and patients must be monitored very closely.

Kevin decided to try the antiviral therapy despite the risk of serious side effects. He felt he had a good chance at arresting his disease because he was infected with the type 2 virus, which responds better to the treatment. His health insurance carrier

ANTIVIRAL SIDE EFFECTS

Interferon administration causes influenza-like symptoms in more than 60% of patients. Other side effects include chronic fatigue, depression, and mood disorders. Increasing the duration of therapy from 6 months to 12 months increases the likelihood of adverse effects. Treatment also may cause insomnia; rash and itching; anorexia; a large decrease in neutrophils (a type of white blood cell); a serious decrease in the number of blood platelets, which are essential for proper blood clotting; and abnormal function of the thyroid gland.

Treatment with ribavirin may cause **hemolytic anemia**. In this condition, there is a decrease in the number of red blood cells in the blood because the cells lyse, or "blow up." It can be a serious condition because red blood cells transport oxygen throughout the body and an insufficient number causes tissues to be oxygen-starved. Ribavirin can also cause birth defects and is not advised in pregnant women. Patients may develop a cough and have difficulty breathing. Rash and itching can also develop, as can insomnia and anorexia.

agreed to cover the very high cost of treatment. Kevin's gamble paid off. His treatment was successful, his blood became virus-free, and he resumed a fairly normal life. However, he would have to be tested regularly for liver function, especially for blood levels of ALT and bilirubin (see Chapter 2), and for the presence of virus in his blood.

WORLDWIDE OCCURRENCE AND PREVENTION

The World Health Organization estimates that about 170 million people alive today are infected with HCV, with about 4 million of them in the United States. About 20% of all acute hepatitis cases are due to HCV, and about 10,000 deaths in the United States each year are the result of chronic hepatitis C. Medical care costs for hepatitis C in this country exceed $600 million each year. Most liver transplants in the United States are given to chronic hepatitis C patients. The number of new infections each year in the United States dropped dramatically from 240,000 in the 1980s to about 25,000 in 2001. Routine screening for HCV in donated blood is primarily responsible for this positive outcome. However, there is concern that increased drug abuse could lead to an increase in HCV in the United States. Worldwide, HCV incidence is increasing. The World Health Organization is working hard to reduce post-transfusion hepatitis C and is promoting education for intravenous drug users.

There is no vaccine for HCV. Prevention requires avoiding the common routes of transmission, which all involve direct introduction of the virus into the blood. Recreational use of intravenous drugs is never wise, but sharing of needles should be avoided. Sharing of other objects that could have infected blood on them, such as razors, toothbrushes, and the straws used to snort cocaine, can also lead to infection if the user has open cuts or sores. Tattooing and body piercing should be done only by someone who practices scrupulous hygiene.

10

Hepatitides E and G

SATYA

Satya was 25 years old and living in Des Moines, Iowa. His parents had emigrated from Bangalore, India, to work at the University of Iowa in Iowa City, Iowa, where he was born and raised. Satya grew up with stories about family in Bangalore but had never been there. He knew his grand-parents were aging, so he took a two-week vacation to visit them and was off to Bangalore.

Satya enjoyed meeting his family, and his grandparents were thrilled. They had only seen pictures of him until now. He learned a lot about himself, his family, and India. He also loved the food! The fresh fruits and vegetables that could be purchased daily in the local open-air market were especially good, and he enjoyed the ritual of the trip to the market and bargaining with the vendors. Satya's visit was a great success and he left for home vowing to go back to India as soon as he could.

One month after his return to Des Moines, Satya became ill. First, he had flu-like symptoms—nausea, vomiting, and fatigue. Then a fever set in, his urine turned dark yellow, his stool became clay-colored, and his eyes yellowed. His doctor suspected hepatitis and did a series of blood tests for hepatitides A, B, and C to identify the specific disease. Satya had been vaccinated for hepatitides A and B as a young child. Test results showed that he had anti-HAV IgG, the antibody for HAV (Chapter 6), and anti-HBs and anti-HBc, antibodies for HBV. There was no anti-HBsAg (Chapter 7). Therefore, Satya was immune to hepatitides A and B, and could not have hepatitis D (Chapter 8). An EIA-2 test result for hepatitis C antibodies was negative (Chapter 9). Satya did not have hepatitis C but clearly had a form of hepatitis. When doctors do not know which virus is causing the disease, but can exclude some, as in Satya's case, they say that the patient has non-A, non-B, non-C, non-D hepatitis (or non-A, B, C, D hepatitis).

Tests for the remaining two hepatitides, E and G, are not routinely available because economical tests have not yet been developed. A friend of Satya's parents, a virologist at the University of Iowa Medical School, was doing research on hepatitis viruses. He was able to check Satya's blood for the immunoglobulins anti-HEV-IgMs and confirmed their presence. Satya had hepatitis E. Satya received the diagnosis about a month after he first became ill and was already recovering from the acute phase of the illness. His symptoms were less severe, and he was able to slowly resume his normal activities. The virologist told Satya that he should expect a complete recovery and then he would be immune to the disease for the rest of his life, since hepatitis E does not have a chronic phase. This is because the immune system can successfully fight this virus.

ABOUT HEV

The hepatitis E virus, HEV, was first identified in India in 1990. It has not been classified, but it has structural similarities to the family of caliciviruses (Figure 10.1). The caliciviruses cause diarrhea in children and adults. Childhood diarrhea is a major cause of infant mortality in many parts of the world. HEV is spherical and the nucleocapsid encloses single-stranded RNA that can serve immediately as messenger RNA (see Chapter 5) when released into the host cytoplasm. It has no envelope.

The immunoglobulins anti-HEV IgM and anti-HEV IgG appear in the blood by the time the icteric phase of the disease begins. These antibodies work effectively to destroy the virus over a period of a few months. The route of newly made enteric viruses is from the bile to the gut, from the gut to the blood, and then from the blood back into uninfected hepatocytes. The presence of strong antibodies in the blood thus catches all the

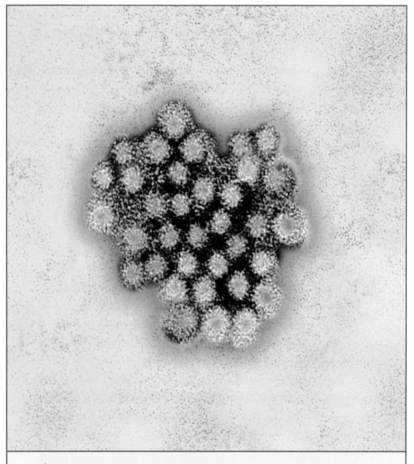

Figure 10.1 This is an electron microscope image of a cluster of caliciviruses known as the Norwalk virus, magnified 80,000 times. This virus causes gastrointestinal (GI) disorders with symptoms such as severe diarrhea and vomiting. The small bumps on each virus are parts of the capsomers that give the virus a characteristic appearance. A good image of HEV is not available, but it is thought that it has a smoother capsid than is seen here.

new virions that would otherwise keep the disease going. Killer T cells take care of the virus inside hepatocytes. Hepatitis E does not have a chronic phase, thanks to the strong humoral (body fluid) response. As a person recovers, anti-HEV IgM slowly disappears from the blood, but anti-HEV IgG remains to provide permanent immunity.

TRANSMISSION OF HEV

Fecal-contaminated water and food is the most common route of transmission. This is probably how Satya was infected. Either the fresh produce he ate so lustily in India was washed with contaminated water, or a vendor was a carrier who did not observe good personal hygiene. Uncooked or partially cooked contaminated shellfish is another route of transmission. Transmission is strictly waterborne. Close person-to-person transmission is unknown.

TREATMENT OF HEV

The immune system does a good job of limiting HEV infection to an acute phase only. A victim can be very uncomfortable while experiencing symptoms and may be unable to engage in normal activities. However, recovery normally occurs within a few months of infection. Only symptoms may be treated to decrease suffering; there is no treatment for the disease itself.

WORLDWIDE OCCURRENCE
AND PREVENTION OF HEV

There is no vaccine for HEV. Clean public water supplies are the most important measure for protection of the public. Good personal hygiene, avoidance of uncooked produce and raw shellfish in areas where HEV is endemic, and drinking bottled water when traveling to areas with high incidence are prudent measures. Pregnant women are more susceptible than others to HEV, especially during their third trimester. Infected pregnant women have a 20% risk of developing fulminant hepatitis. They also have a high risk of premature delivery and a 33% chance that the baby will die. Pregnant women should avoid travel to areas with high incidence of HEV (Figure 10.2).

(continued on page 101)

TRANSMISSION OF VIRUSES BETWEEN DIFFERENT ANIMAL SPECIES

Most viruses have very specific host requirements. However, there are some important cases in which animal-to-human transmission of a virus can cause human disease. The transmission is not necessarily direct, although it can be. Rabies is a good example of direct transmission. A bite from a rabid animal can introduce the virus directly into a person's blood, and the virus can replicate in humans with devastating consequences. Influenza A virus has many forms, but all of them are carried with no ill effect by ducks. Occasionally, a new form of influenza A will be transmitted directly to humans, say by water contaminated by duck feces. Ducks can also directly infect other birds, such as chickens, producing avian flu. Chickens are often ground up for hog meal. Pigs that eat infected chicken meal can develop an influenza that can then be transmitted to humans either by direct contact or by contamination of water with their feces. There is one known case in which a human infected a pig and a flu epidemic among pigs followed.

The SARS virus has caused a great deal of concern world-wide because it causes a very severe infection and could cause a major epidemic or pandemic. SARS means "severe acute respiratory syndrome" and was first described in Asia in 2003. A global outbreak occurred after that, but it has been contained. The virus spreads through the air by close person-to-person contact, meaning that if an infected person is in close proximity to a healthy person, the virus will be present in the air exhaled by the infected person and can be transmitted to a healthy person who inhales that air. It is believed that animals also carry the virus and can spread it to humans through the air or by direct contact with a carcass. Tens of thousands of animals were slaughtered in China after the SARS outbreak because of fear that they could be carriers of the virus. However, at this time, it is not clear whether animal-to-human transfer of the SARS virus is the main method of transmission. The human outbreak may have started this way, but control of the epidemic was achieved mainly by quarantine of infected humans.

Some viruses are transmitted by mosquitoes. The insect itself is not affected by the virus. It takes a blood meal from one animal that has a high virus count in its blood and then bites another animal. The second animal picks up the virus from the digestive fluids of the mosquito. The West Nile virus is a good example of this kind of transmission. Birds and horses are infected by this virus and can become sick and die. Mosquitoes bite birds, horses, and humans. Not only can a female mosquito transfer the virus from an infected bird to a human, but it can pass the virus on to her offspring in her eggs. Mosquito control is a major priority in all areas where West Nile virus has appeared.

The Ebola virus is extremely deadly. It has caused a major decline in the populations of great apes in Africa. It also infects humans and kills 90% of those infected. Humans can acquire the virus by direct contact with an infected ape or ape carcass. The Hantavirus is another example. This virus infects prairie dogs. It can cause serious respiratory inflammation in humans and is acquired by direct contact with the animals or by breathing dust contaminated with infected prairie dog dung. A serious outbreak of this disease occurred in the southwestern United States in 1993.

Certain species of African rats are popular as pets. These rats can be infected by the monkeypox virus, which is similar to the smallpox virus. Rats imported as pets in 2003 infected pet prairie dogs that then infected their owners. The infection causes a blister-like skin rash in humans.

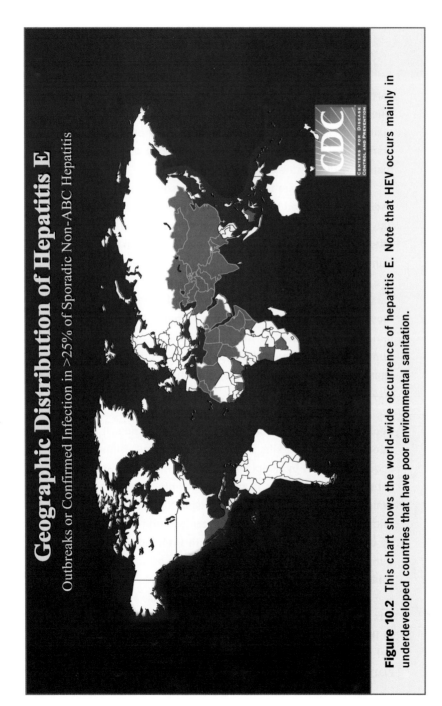

Geographic Distribution of Hepatitis E

Outbreaks or Confirmed Infection in >25% of Sporadic Non-ABC Hepatitis

Figure 10.2 This chart shows the world-wide occurrence of hepatitis E. Note that HEV occurs mainly in underdeveloped countries that have poor environmental sanitation.

(continued from page 97)

HEV is very rare in the United States, Canada, and Western Europe. However, there is some concern that HEV in pigs could infect humans, and this possibility is being watched closely.

Outbreaks of HEV are common in tropical and sub-tropical areas where there is poor sanitation but are rare in temperate areas. Outbreaks tend to occur during the monsoon season after heavy flooding that contaminates wells or when raw sewage gets into a city water treatment plant.

HEV is endemic (Figure 10.2) in Algeria, Bangladesh, Borneo, China, Egypt, Ethiopia, Greece, India, Indonesia, Iran, Ivory Coast, Jordan, Libya, Mexico, Myanmar, Nepal, Nigeria, Pakistan, southern Russia, Somalia, eastern Sudan, and the Gambia. In Egypt, about 60% of adults are positive for anti-HEV IgG. It is thought that children are infected with HEV early in their lives and have no symptoms, like with HAV.

G. B.

G. B. was a young surgeon who contracted a mild case of acute hepatitis in the 1970s. It is not known how G. B. was infected, but it may have occurred when he cut himself with a scalpel during surgery. Tests for hepatitides A and B were negative. This occurred before the identification of HCV, so he was considered to have non-A, non-B hepatitis. His serum was used to inoculate monkeys to identify the virus. This was a standard approach to find new viruses at that time, but the efforts met with no success. Efforts to isolate G. B.'s virus continued for about 20 years until 1995. Then, thanks to more modern techniques, researchers were able to isolate three different viruses from monkey serum. These were named GBV-A, GBV-B, and GBV-C after the surgeon, G. B. It was determined that the first two viruses were specific to the tamarin monkey from which they were isolated, but that GBV-C could be the virus that had caused G. B.'s hepatitis. There had been many reports of non-A, non-E hepatitis, many of which were probably transfusion infections. About the same time, other researchers had isolated a new virus from a human with non-A, non-E hepatitis. They called the new virus hepatitis G virus (HGV). A year later, it was shown that GBV-C and HGV were the same virus.

The symptoms of hepatitis G are very mild versions of the standard acute hepatitis symptoms. Some scientists think that the virus is persistent but does not cause the liver complications of other chronic hepatitis virus infections. HGV is often found together with HCV, but there is no evidence that HGV aggravates the illness the way HDV aggravates an HBV infection. HGV is a bloodborne virus and is transmitted in the same way as HCV. Most experts now believe that HGV is not responsible for any serious acute or chronic hepatitis.

ABOUT HGV

HGV is a flavivirus like HCV, but its genome has little in common with that of HCV. HGV is a genetically distinct virus that contains a single-stranded RNA. It is spherical, and has an envelope. The replication process is probably similar to that of HCV. Structural and nonstructural proteins have been identified, but at present no reliable blood test for HGV antigens or anti-HGV proteins has been developed. Positive identification of HGV requires research laboratory-level testing that is too difficult and expensive for routine use. Little else is known about the virus.

TRANSMISSION OF HGV

Exposure to contaminated blood is the most common route of HGV infection. Post-transfusion hepatitis that still occurs in developed countries that routinely screen donated blood for the hepatitis A–C viruses is thought to be caused by HGV. Newborns can acquire the virus from their mothers, but babies seem to tolerate the virus well and develop immunity without showing symptoms. It is also possible that HGV is transmitted sexually, but there is limited information about this route at this time.

WORLDWIDE OCCURRENCE
AND PREVENTION OF HGV

HGV has been found worldwide, but does not cause epidemics. There is no vaccine for HGV. The same precautions that are used to avoid HCV (see Chapter 9) should be used for HGV. An estimated 30% of people in some regions are infected with HGV, including many drug abusers who are also infected with HCV. One U.S. study found that 18% of non-A, non-B hepatitis patients had HGV, and 80% of those patients also had HCV. Another U.S. study found that about 15% of chronic hepatitis C patients also are infected with HGV.

The story of HGV is still being written. It has actually been only a short time since the virus was first identified. The effects of a pure HGV infection have been difficult to study because it is so closely associated with HCV. Although experts now believe HGV is not an important cause of acute or chronic hepatitis or a serious threat to public health, further study of the virus and its effects on humans may eventually change that view. One very practical reason for continuing research on this virus is the question of whether or not to screen donated blood for HGV. If HGV causes no serious or long-term effects, then it would be a tragic waste of donated blood if screening were implemented and infected blood discarded. Similarly, it could be a tragic error to assume that the question is settled and stop research on the medical consequences of HGV infection.

11

Conclusion

MIKE REVISITED

We began this book with the story of Mike, who had contracted viral hepatitis, but interrupted his story to explore the various kinds of hepatitis. Mike's doctor had ordered serological tests to check for hepatitides A, B, and C. He knew Mike had been vaccinated, but sometimes the vaccinations don't work. Immunity to HAV is thought to last a lifetime, but HBV immunity can disappear after 10 years or more in some people. The results showed that Mike was still immune to HAV and HBV. The EIA-2 test for anti-HCV antibodies was positive, and this finding was confirmed with an RIBA-2 test (see Chapters 4 and 9). A 6-month follow-up showed that Mike was still HCV-positive. The likelihood was that he would develop chronic hepatitis C. Liver function tests were then done, and Mike's serum ALT level was high. This measurement provided an important baseline for monitoring the progress of Mike's disease.

The liver specialist to whom Mike was referred wanted to see him every 6 months to check on the progress of the infection. Serological tests and liver enzyme measurements were done. On Mike's first visit, the specialist also checked the virus genotype because this information can influence the treatment. Mike had HCV type 1b—common among drug abusers in the United States. Unfortunately, it is the most difficult type to treat.

Mike talked to the specialist about how he could have acquired the virus. This time, he was honest about his one-time experiment with cocaine. The doctor explained that it was possible to acquire the virus this way, although it is not a common route. Dirty needles used by intravenous drug abusers are the most common source of infection in the United States. In Mike's case, he inserted a snorting straw into his nose, where it may have either scraped the soft tissue in his nose and caused some minor bleeding or simply rubbed against an open sore. This blood contact must have happened at least twice in Mike's case. First, it happened to the carrier, who might not have noticed such a minor injury. Then, it happened to Mike, who also didn't notice his own injury. The doctor suggested that Mike talk to the three other people who shared the straw that night and urge them to be checked for HCV.

Mike was too young to be a candidate for the PEG-INF plus ribavirin treatment (see Chapter 9) because children and young adults under age 19 can develop serious side effects. His symptoms had disappeared and he was living a normal life, except that he had to see the liver specialist every 6 months for testing. Three years later, Mike's serum ALT levels were showing a pattern of consistent increase and his serum albumin level was decreasing. This is a red flag for serious liver damage, but it does not prove that the disease is progressing. As a precaution, the specialist ordered a liver biopsy. This procedure is not routine because it is expensive and unpleasant to undergo. However, it is the one reliable way of judging the extent of liver damage and the likelihood of future liver damage. The biopsy showed that Mike's disease had caused significant liver damage (Figure 11.1) and that the disease was likely to progress to cirrhosis.

By this time, Mike was old enough to be eligible for PEG-INF plus ribavirin therapy. His liver was still intact enough that it could continue to function well if HCV replication was arrested. He was young and otherwise healthy, and the disease was threatening to get worse. If the disease was left unchecked, Mike would be likely to develop cirrhosis and ultimately need a liver transplant (if he could get one). The odds of success for this therapy were only fair, given that Mike was infected with the type 1b virus. However, the benefits far outweighed the risks in Mike's mind. He agreed to try it.

Mike's course of treatment was planned to continue for one year, with weekly injections of PEG-INF and a daily oral

Figure 11.1 This light microscope image of a human liver sample infected with hepatitis (magnified 200 times) has numerous darkly stained irregular structures that are called plaques. Plaques are formed when infected hepatocytes are destroyed by killer T cells. Accumulation of plaques leads to cirrhosis and ultimately to liver failure. A large number of plaques seen in a liver biopsy would suggest that serious liver failure is likely to occur in the future.

dose of ribavirin. His initial response was typical: fatigue, nausea, rash, and irritability on occasion. All this would have been bearable, but 4 months after the start of therapy, Mike's bloodwork provided some ominous information. He was developing hemolytic anemia, a decrease in the number of red blood cells caused by the cells lysing, or "blowing up." It can be a serious condition because the red blood cells transport oxygen throughout the body and having too few of them causes tissues to be oxygen-starved. Mike noticed that he was bleeding from his gums after brushing his teeth. Mike's blood platelet level was dropping to dangerously low levels (see Chapter 9). Platelets are an essential part of the blood-clotting process, and a lack of platelets places a person at high risk for bleeding to death. The treatment was stopped.

Mike's options for dealing with his disease were now much more limited. He could try another treatment course in a year or so, but in the meantime, liver damage would be progressing; he could do nothing and take the chance that he would not develop cirrhosis; or, he could be placed on the waiting list for a liver transplant. The decision was made to place Mike on the transplant waiting list, but only if another treatment course, which was adjusted to deal with the complications he had suffered, failed. Mike is still awaiting the outcome.

SUMMARY

Viral hepatitis proceeds through two stages (see Chapter 2). All forms have an acute stage, but only hepatitides B, C, and D have the second, or chronic, stage. The acute stage has four phases, not all of which are always observable. The incubation phase starts with the entry of virus into the body and is always symptom-free. However, the virus replicates actively at this time, is present in the blood, and, for enteric viruses, is shed in the feces. Carriers are most infectious during this incubation phase of acute hepatitis when they don't even know they are infected. The prodromal phase begins with the onset of symptoms, if any occur; otherwise, it begins when antibodies to the viral antigens first appear in the blood. Three to 10 days later, the icteric phase begins and lasts about 4 weeks. Jaundice may develop, but in most patients it does not. Serum antibodies climb to some of their highest levels during this phase. Finally, the recovery phase sets in if the immune system is able to defeat the virus. Recovery lasts 4 to 8 weeks. Symptoms fade away slowly and the patient returns to normal. Serum antibodies for the virus remain to provide permanent immunity against reinfection.

Chronic hepatitis begins when there is evidence of active infection for 6 or more months. The chronic stage has three phases, but these do not occur in a one-time sequence. The phases can recur repeatedly. The replicative phase can last up to 3 years. The virus replicates actively, with significant viremia. The disease is most contagious during this phase. The seroconversion phase is the period during which the immune system produces antibodies and aggressively attacks infected cells. A change in the antibodies is seen in the blood, and serum ALT levels can be high because of the destruction of up to 10% of liver cells per year. Finally, the nonreplicative phase sets in, during which the virus is inactive and almost disappears from the blood; it is lying in wait within host cells. However, a new replicative phase can arise at any time to initiate a new cycle or not at all.

All forms of hepatitis have symptoms in common, most of which are experienced primarily in the acute stage of the disease. It is significant that many people never experience symptoms or do so late in the course of a chronic infection. This means that the disease can proceed to destroy the liver without the victim knowing it until it is too late. It also means that spread of hepatitis by carriers is a serious public health problem.

The most common symptoms are flu-like—nausea, vomiting, abdominal pain, fever, muscle aches and pains, and fatigue. Anorexia can also develop, followed by jaundice and itching. Fatigue may persist for months. Itching always develops in the recovery phase of the acute stage, if at all. Symptoms usually recede by the end of the acute stage, but they may recur during the chronic stage. Fatigue is probably the most common chronic-stage symptom and may or may not be disabling.

Tables 1.1, 1.2, and 1.3 in the appendix provide a quick summary of the pertinent facts on the characteristic of each disease, the transmission routes, and the diagnostic serology unique to each form of viral hepatitis therapy. They are not a substitute for a more thorough understanding.

Appendix

Table 1.1 Key Facts About Hepatitis Viruses

VIRUS	CLASS	TRANSMISSION	NUCLEIC ACID	ENVELOPE	CHRONIC PHASE	INCUBATION TIME (WEEKS)
A	Waterborne	Fecal/oral	RNA	No	No	2–7
B	Bloodborne	Fecal/oral	DNA	Yes	Yes	6–23
C	Bloodborne	Parenteral	RNA	Yes	Yes	2–25
D	Bloodborne	Parenteral	RNA, partial circle	Yes, comes from HBV	Yes, requires chronic HBV	2–8
E	Waterborne	Fecal/oral	RNA	No	No	2–9
G	Bloodborne	Parenteral	RNA	Yes	Yes	Unknown

Terms:

- **Waterborne** refers to enteric viruses (viruses that enter the blood from the gut) that are transmitted primarily by drinking contaminated water.

- **Bloodborne** refers to viruses that are transmitted by direct entry into the blood and can survive only in blood.

- **Fecal/oral** transmission means that the virus is shed in the feces and is often acquired by way of the mouth by drinking contaminated water or placing contaminated objects in the mouth.

- **Parenteral** transmission means that the virus can enter the blood by all possible routes except the gut.

Table 1.2 Viral Transmission Routes

ROUTE	HAV	HBV	HCV	HDV	HEV	HGV
Contaminated food	Yes	No	No	No	Yes	No
Contaminated drinking water	Yes	No	No	No	Yes	No
Raw shellfish	Yes	No	No	No	Yes	No
Within family	Yes	Yes	Possible	Yes	Yes	No
Injectable drug abuse	Possible	Yes	Yes	Yes	?	?
Blood transfusion	Rare	Yes	Yes	Yes	Rare	?
Sexual contact	Yes	Yes	Rare	Yes	?	?
Oral contact	No	Yes	Rare	?	No	?
Mother/baby	No	Yes	Rare	No	?	?

Terms:

- "?" means that not enough is known about the topic.
- **Possible** means that transmission can occur theoretically, but that the route has not been established.
- **Rare** means that the route has been established, but it is unusual.
- **Within family** refers to any possible ways that family members come into contact, such as sharing eating utensils, razors, toothbrushes, or food handling.
- **Sexual contact** refers to sexual intercourse, including anal intercourse.
- **Oral contact** refers to kissing or oral/anal sex.
- **Mother/baby** refers to transmission to the newborn from the mother's vaginal fluids during birth.

Appendix

Table 1.3 Diagnostic Serology[*]

TYPE	STAGE	SERUM ANTIGENS AND ANTIBODIES
Hepatitis A	Acute phase only	Anti-HAV-IgM, anti-HAV-IgG
Hepatitis B	Acute phase	HBsAg, anti-HBc-IgM, anti-HBs-IgG, anti-HBc-IgG
	Chronic phase	HBsAg, HBeAg, anti-HBc-IgG, HBV-DNA
Hepatitis C	Acute and chronic phases	Anti-HCc-IgG, plus other anti-HCV antibodies
Hepatitis D	Acute coinfection	HBsAg, anti-HBc-IgG, anti-HD-IgM, HDAg, HbsAg
	Acute superinfection	Anti-HBe-IgM, anti-HD-IgM, HBsAg, anti-HBe-IgM
	Chronic	Other anti-HDV antibodies
Hepatitis E	Acute	Anti-HEV-IgM early, anti-HEV-IgG late
Hepatitis G	All stages	HGV-RNA

[*] The table summarizes the serum antigens (Ag) and antibodies (Ig or the prefix anti-) that can be found by serological tests for each form of hepatitis. Bear in mind that these substances appear and disappear, depending on the stage of the disease as well as the phase of each stage, and are never all present at the same time.

Acute—Starting suddenly and not lasting long.

Acute viral hepatitis—Initial short-term stage of hepatitis.

Alanine aminotransferase—Enzyme involved in the normal chemical processing of the amino acid alanine, which converts it to carbon dioxide and water and provides useful energy for the cell.

ALT—See **Alanine aminotransferase**.

Antibodies—Proteins produced by the immune system in response to antigens to fight a foreign body.

Antigens—Proteins that signal the presence of a foreign substance to the immune system.

Apoptosis—A pattern of cell death affecting individual cells.

B cells—Cells of the immune system that are responsible for humoral (body fluid) immunity.

Bile—A yellow to green-brown fluid secreted by the liver that is necessary for the digestion of fats.

Bile duct, hepatic—A tube that conveys bile from the liver.

Bilirubin—Orange-yellow bile pigment, which is a product of the breakdown of red blood cells.

Bloodborne—Transmitted only through the blood.

Budding—Process in which a virus pushes outward on the host cell membrane and the membrane folds around the capsid.

Canaliculi—Very small vessels.

Capsid—Protective protein coat for a viral nucleic acid.

Capsomer—Protein subunits that make up a capsid.

Carrier—A person who is infected but shows no symptoms and, in the case of hepatitis, can spread the virus.

Chronic hepatitis—Long-standing hepatitis infection.

Cirrhosis—A form of advanced liver degeneration.

Clinical disease—An illness that causes symptoms that require treatment by a medical professional.

Clinical sign—An abnormality caused by a disease that can be discovered by a doctor's examination of a patient.

Glossary

Coagulation—The process of blood clotting.

Coinfection—Infection by two different microbes at the same time.

Complement proteins—Proteins produced by the liver that help antibodies attack foreign substances.

Core antigen—An antigen in the viral capsid that is part of the "core" or essential structure of the virus.

Cytoplasm—Substance that makes up the interior of a cell.

DNA—Deoxyribonucleic acid; a nucleic acid molecule that carries coded genetic information.

Endemic—Common or always present in a specific geographical area.

Enteric—Within or pertaining to the intestine.

Envelope—A membrane that encloses the nucleocapsid of some viruses.

Epitope—Small structural part of an antigen, which determines when a foreign substance is present.

Fulminant hepatitis—Sudden, extremely severe liver inflammation.

Genotype—Genetic constitution of an individual organism.

Helper T cell—Type of immune cell. Helper T cells act as guardians of the body and activate killer T and B cells.

Hemolytic anemia—An abnormal decrease in red blood cells, caused by their destruction.

Hepatic artery—The artery that supplies the liver with blood.

Hepatic encephalopathy—Brain disorder caused by a shrinking, malfunctioning liver.

Hepatic vein—Any of the veins that carries blood brought by the hepatic artery and the portal veins away from the liver. Humans usually have three hepatic veins.

Hepatocellular carcinoma—Cancer of the liver cells.

Hepatocytes—Cells that take materials from the blood, modify them, and deliver them along with new materials back to the blood.

Hepatomegaly—Enlarged liver.

Humoral—Pertaining to body fluids.

Humoral response—An immune response that involves only antibodies in the body fluids.

Icosahedron—A polygon with 20 sides.

Icteric phase—Phase of hepatitis infection in which the skin, urine, stools, and sclerae (the whites of the eyes) turn yellow.

Immunity—The state of being unsusceptible to a particular condition or disease.

Immunoglobulin—Any of five classes of structurally distinct antibodies in the serum.

Incidence—The number of new cases of a disease per year for a specified number of people.

Incubation phase—Span of time from the initial infection until the appearance of symptoms.

Inflammation—A protective response of tissues to injury. It is characterized by pain, redness, swelling, and heat.

Interferon—Specialized protein produced by some cells that "interferes" with viral replication.

Jaundice—A condition of high bilirubin with yellowing of the skin.

Killer T cells—Immune cells that are activated by helper T cells that identify, attack, and destroy infected cells.

Liver biopsy—The process of taking a living tissue sample from a patient's liver for examination with a microscope. Samples may be obtained by brushing the surface of the tissue, or cutting a piece of tissue off with a scalpel or scissors. A liver biopsy is done with special needle and requires minor surgery and local anesthesia. There is a small risk of damage to the lungs or gallbladder, as well as a risk of infection.

Lobes, hepatic—Portions of the liver.

Lobules—Small lobes.

Lysis—A sudden opening-up of a cell to release its contents, something like an explosion; lysis kills cells.

Macrophages—Large cells that originate in the bone marrow and are found throughout the body. They are scavengers of tissue debris and dead cells.

Glossary

Major histocompatibility complex (MHC)—A special protein on the surface of cells that holds onto epitopes that can be recognized by killer T cells.

Microbe—Any very small organism such as a bacterium or virus that does not have a nucleus.

Nonreplicative phase—Period during which the virus stops reproducing itself and viremia has decreased to a minimal level.

Nucleic acid—Compound within a cell that is involved in determination and transmission of genetic characteristics. There are two kinds: DNA and RNA.

Nucleocapsid—Viral nucleic acid that is enclosed by a capsid.

Outbreak—Sudden increase of disease in a small area.

Pandemic—A wide epidemic that spreads over continents.

Parenteral transmission—Introduction of substances into the body by injection or direct exposure to an open wound.

Pegylated—Man-made type of interferon, used to treat hepatitis C infection.

Phagocytes—Cells specialized for engulfing and destroying other cells and foreign substances.

Phagocytosis—The mechanism by which phagocytes engulf substances.

Polyprotein—A protein composed of many different proteins linked together end to end.

Portal vein—Vein that supplies blood drained from the intestines to the liver.

Prevalence—Number of all cases of a disease, new and old, per year in a given population.

Prodromal phase—Period of onset of disease symptoms.

Proliferation—Cell division, multiplication, and growth.

Proteins—Molecules made up of specific sequences of amino acids that are chemically linked. They are the functional and structural units of cells.

Recovery phase—The final disease phase of an acute infection in which the immune system ultimately overcomes the virus and symptoms fade away.

Regenerate—Rebuild and restore the original structure and function of a damaged tissue, starting with only a remnant of the original tissue, without any external help.

Replicative phase—Period during which the virus reproduces itself and infects healthy cells.

RNA—Ribonucleic acid; a nucleic acid molecule that is involved directly in protein synthesis.

Satellite virus—A virus with a capsid that requires the help of another virus to reproduce. Because it is less complete than the helper virus and is always found in its presence, it is referred to as a satellite.

Self-limited—When the body's immune system defeats a viral infection.

Seroconversion phase—Period during which the immune system attacks and destroys about 10% of infected liver cells each year; usually characterized by no symptoms and less viremia.

Serum—The thin liquid part of whole blood that remains after all blood cells and clotting materials are removed.

Sinus—A cavity, channel, or hollow.

Sinusoids—Small sinuses.

Superinfection—An infection by a new microbe that occurs after an earlier infection has occurred and is in a chronic phase.

Symptoms—Evidence of disease that is reported by the patient, such as a headache or fatigue.

T lymphocytes—White blood cells that are present at high levels in special organs called lymph nodes and are produced in the thymus gland.

Transcription—Process of copying or transcribing the codons in a gene to start synthesis of the protein encoded by that gene.

Viral nucleic acid—Nucleic acid molecule present in a virus that carries coded genetic information that allows for the reproduction of viruses similar to itself.

Viremia—Viruses in the blood.

Virion—The virus structure that exits a host cell and is able to infect other cells.

Bibliography

BOOKS

Bader, T. F. *Viral Hepatitis. Practical Evaluation and Treatment,* 3rd ed. Cambridge, MA: Hogrefe and Huber, 2001.

Koff, Raymond S., and George Y. Wu. *Chronic Viral Hepatitis. Diagnosis and Therapeutics.* Totowa, NJ: Humana Press, 2001.

Tibbs, Christopher J. *Clinicians' Guide to Viral Hepatitis.* London: Arnold Publishers, 2001.

Wagner, E. K., and M. J. Hewlett. *Basic Virology.* Ames, IA: Blackwell Science, 1999.

Worman, Howard J. *The Liver Disorders Sourcebook.* New York: McGraw-Hill, 1999.

WEBSITES

The Bad Bug Book
http://www.cfsan.fda.gov/~mow/intro.html

The Centers for Disease Control and Prevention on hepatitis
http://www.cdc.gov/ncidod/diseases/hepatitis/index.htm

Critical clinical facts about hepatitis
http://www.hopkins-id.edu/diseases/hepatitis/hepatitis.html

Current research papers
http://www.cumc.columbia.edu/dept/gi/disliv.html

Diseases of the liver
http://www.euroliver.org/englishbri/entree.htm

Hepatitis Foundation International
http://www.hepfi.org/index.html

The hepatitis viruses
http://gsbs.utmb.edu/microbook/ch070.htm

National Institutes of Health on hepatitis
http://www.nlm.nih.gov/medlineplus/hepatitis.html

Technical resource
http://hepatitis-central.com

Virus structure and taxonomy
http://www.tulane.edu/~dmsander/WWW/335/VirusGroups.html

Everson, Gregory T., and Hedy Weinberg. *Living with Hepatitis B: A Survivor's Guide.* Long Island City, NY: Hatherleigh Press, 2002.

———. *Living with Hepatitis C: A Survivor's Guide,* 3rd ed. Long Island City, NY: Hatherleigh Press, 2002.

Palmer, Melissa. *Guide to Hepatitis & Liver Disease: What You Need to Know.* New York: Avery Publishing Group, 2004.

Parr, Elizabeth. *I'm Glad You're Not Dead: A Liver Transplant Story.* Gloucester, MA: Journey Publishing, 2000.

Radetsky, P. *The Invisible Invaders: Viruses and the Scientists Who Pursue Them.* Boston: Little, Brown and Company, 1991.

Regis, E. *Virus Ground Zero. Stalking the Killer Viruses with the Centers for Disease Control.* New York: Pocket Books, 1996.

Zimmerman, Barry E., and David J. Zimmerman. *Killer Germs.* New York: McGraw-Hill/Contemporary Books, 1996.

Websites

The Euroliver Foundation educational materials about liver diseases
http://www.hepatitis.org/accueilangl.htm

Fatigue as a symptom of hepatitis
http://www.wrongdiagnosis.com/sym/fatigue.htm

History of the discovery of virus structure by the Department of Molecular
Microbiology, Washington University School of Medicine, St. Louis
http://medschool.wustl.edu/~virology

Links to every possible question you may have about viruses called "All the
Virology on the WWW" by Professor David Sander of Tulane University
http://www.tulane.edu/~dmsander/garryfavweb.html

The Liver Foundation educational materials
http://www.liverfoundation.org/db-home/articles

Many links to sites devoted to hepatitis
http://www.hepatitis-c.de/linkse.htm

National Institutes of Health discussion of the immune system
http://www.niaid.nih.gov/final/immun/immun.htm

National Library of Medicine information
http://www.nlm.nih.gov/medlineplus/hepatitis.html

The World Health Organization site for hepatitis
http://www.who.int/health_topics/hepatitis/en/

Index

Index

Index

Picture Credits

9: © Peter Lamb
19: Courtesy Public Health Image Library (PHIL), CDC
26: © Peter Lamb
27: © Peter Lamb
30: © Peter Lamb
35: University of Alabama, Department of Pathology
37: University of Alabama, Department of Pathology
38: University of Alabama, Department of Pathology
41: © Peter Lamb
42: © Peter Lamb
46: © Peter Lamb
50: © Peter Lamb

51: © Peter Lamb
53: © Peter Lamb
60: © Peter Lamb
63: © Peter Lamb
69: © Peter Lamb
71: © Peter Lamb
77: Courtesy the Centers for Disease Control and Prevention (CDC)
80: Courtesy CDC
82: Courtesy CDC
89: Courtesy CDC
90: Courtesy PHIL, CDC
96: © Science VU/Visuals Unlimited
100: Courtesy CDC
106: © Michael Abbey/Visuals Unlimited

Cover: © Gopal Murti/Visuals Unlimited

Hepsera is a registered trademark of Gilead Sciences, Inc.

About the Author

Lyle W. Horn earned a Ph.D. from The Johns Hopkins University in 1970. He taught medical and dental students, graduate students, and undergraduate students in pharmacy, physical therapy, and nursing for 30 years. He has conducted research in his own laboratory, at the Woods Hole Marine Biological Laboratory, and at the National Institutes of Health. He has published original research articles in many scientific journals.

Dr. Horn is retired from teaching and research and is living with his wife, two greyhounds, a chow chow, and four cats in an early 19th-century farmhouse in central Pennsylvania, which he is busy restoring. He also does scientific consulting, medical writing and editing, and community service.

About the Editor

The late I. Edward Alcamo was a Distinguished Teaching Professor of Microbiology at the State University of New York at Farmingdale. Alcamo studied biology at Iona College in New York and earned his M.S. and Ph.D. degrees in microbiology at St. John's University, also in New York. He had taught at Farmingdale for over 30 years. In 2000, Alcamo won the Carski Award for Distinguished Teaching in Microbiology, the highest honor for microbiology teachers in the United States. He was a member of the American Society for Microbiology, the National Association of Biology Teachers, and the American Medical Writers Association. Alcamo authored numerous books on the subjects of microbiology, AIDS, and DNA technology as well as the award-winning textbook *Fundamentals of Microbiology*, now in its sixth edition.